Governor Phillip
to
Botany Bay

Arthur Phillip Esq.

ANECDOTES OF GOVERNOR PHILLIP.

Arthur Phillip is one of those officers, who, like Drake, Dampier, and Cook, has raised himself by his merit and his services, to distinction and command. His father was Jacob Phillip, a native of Frankfort, in Germany, who having settled in England, maintained his family and educated his son by teaching the languages. His mother was Elizabeth Breach, who married for her first husband, Captain Herbert of the navy, a kinsman of Lord Pembroke. Of her marriage with Jacob Phillip, was her son, Arthur, born in the parish of Allhallows, Bread-street, within the city of London, on the 11th of October, 1738.

Being designed for a seafaring life, he was very properly sent to the school of Greenwich, where he received an education suitable to his early propensities. At the age of sixteen, he began his maritime career, under the deceased Captain Michael Everet of the navy, at the commencement of hostilities, in 1755: and at the same time that he learned the rudiments of his profession under that able officer, he partook with him in the early misfortunes, and subsequent glories of the seven years war. Whatever opulence Phillip acquired from the capture of the Havannah, certain it is, that, at the age of twenty-three, he there was made a Lieutenant into the Stirling-castle, on the 7th of June, 1761, by Sir George Pococke, an excellent judge of naval accomplishments.

But of nautical exploits, however they may raise marine officers, there must be an end. Peace, with its blessings, was restored in 1763. And Phillip now found leisure to marry; and to settle at Lyndhurst, in the New Forest, where he amused himself with farming, and like other country gentlemen, discharged assiduously those provincial offices, which, however unimportant, occupy respectably the owners of land, who, in this island, require no office to make them important.

But sailors, like their own element, are seldom at rest. Those occupations, which pleased Phillip while they were new, no longer pleased him when they became familiar. And he hastened to offer his skill and his services to Portugal when it engaged in warfare with Spain. His offer was readily accepted, because such skill and services were necessary amidst an arduous struggle with a too powerful opponent. And, such was his conduct and such his success, that when the recent interference of France, in 1778, made it his duty to fight for his king, and to defend his country, the Portugueze court regretted his departure, but applauded his motive.

His return was doubtless approved by those who, knowing his value, could advance his rank: For he was made master and commander into the Basilisk fireship, on the 2d of September, 1779. But in her he had little opportunity of displaying his zeal, or of adding to his fame. This step, however, led him up to a higher situation; and he was made post-captain into the Ariadne frigate, on the 13th of November, 1781, when he was upwards of three and forty. This is the great epoch in the lives of our naval officers, because it is from this that they date their rank. In the Ariadne, he had little time for active adventures, or for gainful prizes, being appointed to the Europe of sixty-four guns, on the 23d of December, 1781. During the memorable year 1782, Phillip promoted its enterprises, and shared in its glories. And in January, 1783, he sailed with a reinforcement to the East Indies, where superior bravery contended against superior force, till the policy of our negotiators put an end to unequal hostilities by a necessary peace.

The activity, or the zeal of Phillip, was now turned to more peaceful objects. And when it was determined to form a settlement on that part of New Holland, denominated New South Wales, he was thought of as a proper officer to conduct an enterprize, which required professional knowledge, and habitual prudence. His equipment, his voyage, and his settlement, in the other hemisphere, will be found in the following volume. When the time shall arrive that the European settlers on Sydney Cove demand their historian, these authentic anecdotes of their pristine legislator will be sought for as curious, and considered as important.

ERRATA (These have been corrected in this eBook)

Page, line

1, 15, for enterprizes, read enterprises.

13, penult. for only fifty, read an hundred.

Ibid. ult. for Penryn, read Penrhyn.

75, 7, for Surprize, read Surprise.

87, 14, after 17, dele th.

96, 13, for into, read in.

149, 10, for Kangooroo, read Kanguroo. The orthography of a word derived only from oral sound is in some degree arbitrary; but it ought to be consistant. The plates, by mistake, have Kangooroo. 185, 14, for it were were, read if it were.

203, 3, for Fobn, read Thomas.

213, 10, for four, read forty.

228, 23, bis, for Macauley, read Macaulay.

231, 15, for Patri, read Pabi.
252, Margin, for May, read June.
253, Ditto.
255, Margin, for July, read June.
256, Ditto.
232, 18, for Taha, read Toha.
242, 9, for who, read whom.
246, 25, for veer'd, read near'd.

N. B. Some of the early impressions of the plates have erroneously Wulpine Oppossum for Vulpine Opossum. After a few were work'd off the fault was perceived, and corrected.

ADVERTISEMENT.

The arrangement of materials in this volume being in some respects less perfect than might be wished, it is necessary that something should be said to obviate any imputation of negligence. The truth will be the best, and, as it ought, the only apology. The official papers of Governor Phillip, which were liberally communicated by Government, formed at first our principal source of intelligence. These, from their nature, could contain but little information on subjects of natural history, and many other points, concerning which the curiosity of every reader would naturally be excited. The efforts of the publisher to give satisfaction to the public in these respects produced a gradual influx of materials; and the successive arrival of different vessels from the Indian seas, occasioned additions to the work, which made it necessary to engrave new plates. While, therefore, the completion of the book was anxiously pressed by many who were eager to possess it, that desirable point has constantly been deferred by the communications of those who were studious to render it more valuable; and the word Finis, has seemed to fly from us, like Italy before the wandering Trojans. From the combination of these circumstances it has arisen, that every separate part has been hurried on in the execution; and yet, in the finishing of the whole, more time has elapsed, than would have been necessary to complete a much more ample volume. The defects that proceed from these causes, it is hoped, the reader will forgive, and accept with complacency a volume in which, it is confidently hoped, nothing material has been omitted that is connected with its principal object, the formation of a settlement promising both glory and advantage to this country; in which several important discoveries are announced; no small accession is made to the stores of natural history; and interesting notices are communicated of countries visited before, and persons in whose fate the public has long felt an interest.

The publisher thinks it his duty, in this place, to return thanks to the following noblemen and gentlemen, for their kind assistance and free communications. The Marquis of Salisbury, Viscount Sydney, Lord Hood, Sir Joseph Banks, Bart. Mr. Rose, Mr. Nepean, Mr. Stephens, Sir Charles Middleton, Sir Andrew Snape Hammond, Mr. Dalrymple, and Mr. Chalmers: but, to Mr. Latham particularly, the most grateful acknowledgements are due, for having furnished many drawings and accurate descriptions, which stamp a value on the natural history contained in this work, and must for ever render it an object of attention to all lovers of that science: and to Lieutenant Shortland, Lieutenant Watts, and Captain Marshall, of the *Scarborough* transport, the public owe whatever important discoveries and useful knowledge may be found in their journals, which they communicated with a disinterestedness that the publisher will be always happy to acknowledge.

ACCOUNT OF THE VIGNETTE.

The elegant vignette in the title-page, was engraved from a medallion which the ingenious Mr. Wedge-wood caused to be modelled from a small piece of clay brought from Sydney Cove. The clay proves to be of a fine texture, and will be found very useful for the manufactory of earthern ware. The design is allegorical; it represents Hope encouraging Art and Labour, under the influence of Peace, to pursue the employments necessary to give security and happiness to an infant settlement. The following verses upon the same subject, and in allusion to the medallion, were written by the author of The Botanic Garden, and will speak more powerfully for themselves than any encomium we could bestow.

VISIT OF HOPE TO SYDNEY-COVE, NEAR BOTANY-BAY.

Where Sydney Cove her lucid bosom swells,
Courts her young navies, and the storm repels;
High on a rock amid the troubled air
HOPE stood sublime, and wav'd her golden hair;
Calm'd with her rosy smile the tossing deep,

And with sweet accents charm'd the winds to sleep;
To each wild plain she stretch'd her snowy hand,
High-waving wood, and sea-encircled strand.
"Hear me," she cried, "ye rising Realms! record
"Time's opening scenes, and Truth's unerring word.--
"There shall broad streets their stately walls extend,
"The circus widen, and the crescent bend;
"There, ray'd from cities o'er the cultur'd land,
"Shall bright canals, and solid roads expand.--
"There the proud arch, Colossus-like, bestride
"Yon glittering streams, and bound the chasing tide;
"Embellish'd villas crown the landscape-scene,
"Farms wave with gold, and orchards blush between.--
"There shall tall spires, and dome-capt towers ascend,
"And piers and quays their massy structures blend;
"While with each breeze approaching vessels glide,
"And northern treasures dance on every tide!"--
Then ceas'd the nymph--tumultuous echoes roar,
And JOY's loud voice was heard from shore to shore--
Her graceful steps descending press'd the plain,
And PEACE, and ART, and LABOUR, join'd her train.

VIEW of the FLEET and ESTABLISHMENT sent out with GOVERNOR PHILLIP to NEW SOUTH WALES.

Captain ARTHUR PHILLIP of the Navy, Governor and Commander in Chief of the territory of New South Wales, and of his Majesty's ships and vessels employed on that coast.

Major Robert Ross, Lieutenant Governor.

Richard Johnson, Chaplain.
Andrew Miller, Commissary.
David Collins, Judge Advocate.
John Long, Adjutant.
James Furzer, Quarter-Master.
*George *Alexander*, Provost Martial.
John White, Surgeon.
Thomas Arndell, Assistant Ditto.
William Balmain, Ditto Ditto.

[* This Gentleman did not go]
His Majesty's ship *Sirius*,
Captain Arthur Phillip.
Captain John Hunter.

His Majesty's armed tender *Supply*,
Lieutenant H. L. Ball.
Six transports carrying the convicts.

Alexander 210 men convicts. women convicts.
Scarborough 210 men convicts.
Friendship 80 men convicts. 24
Charlotte 100 men convicts. 24
Prince of Wales -- -- 100
Lady Penrhyn -- -- 102

Each transport had a detachment of marines on board.
Three store ships:
The *Golden Grove*, *Fishburn*, and *Borrowdale*;
With provisions, implements for husbandry, cloathing,
etc. for the convicts.

Lieutenant John Shortland, agent for the transports.
The garrison is formed from the marines.

Chapter I.

Public utility of voyages--Peculiar circumstances of this--New Holland properly a continent--Reasons for fixing our settlement there--Transportation to America, its origin, advantages, and cessation--Experiments made--The present plan adopted--Disadvantages of other expedients.

From voyages undertaken expressly for the purpose of discovery, the public naturally looks for information of various kinds: and it is a fact which we cannot but contemplate with pleasure, that by the excellent publications subsequent to such enterprises, very considerable additions have been made, during the present reign, to our general knowledge of the globe, of the various tribes by which it is peopled, and of the animals and vegetables to which it gives support.

An expedition occasioned by motives of legislative policy, carried on by public authority, and concluded by a fixed establishment in a country very remote, not only excites an unusual interest concerning the fate of those sent out, but promises to lead us to some points of knowledge which, by the former mode, however judiciously employed, could not have been attained. A transient visit to the coast of a great continent cannot, in the nature of things, produce a complete information respecting its inhabitants, productions, soil, or climate: all which when contemplated by resident observers, in every possible circumstance of variation, though they should be viewed with less philosophical acuteness, must yet gradually become more fully known: Errors, sometimes inseparable from hasty observation, will then be corrected by infallible experience; and many objects will present themselves to view, which before had escaped notice, or had happened to be so situated that they could not be observed.

The full discovery of the extent of New Holland, by our illustrious navigator, Capt. Cook, has formed a singular epocha in geography; a doubt having arisen from it, whether to a land of such magnitude the name of island or that of continent may more properly be applied. To this question it may be answered, that though the etymology of the word island,* and of others synonymous to it, points out only a land surrounded by the sea, or by any water, (in which sense the term is applicable even to the largest portions of the habitable globe) yet it is certain that, in the usual acceptation, an island is conceived to signify a land of only moderate extent, surrounded by the sea.** To define at what point of magnitude precisely, a country so situated shall begin to be a continent, could not answer any purpose of utility; but the best and clearest rule for removing the doubt appears to be the following: As long as the peculiar advantages of an insular situation can be enjoyed by the inhabitants of such a country, let it have the title of an island; when it exceeds those limits let it be considered as a continent. Now the first and principal advantage of an island, is that of being capable of a convenient union under one government, and of deriving thence a security from all external attacks, except by sea. In lands of very great magnitude such an union is difficult, if not impracticable, and a distinction founded on this circumstance, is therefore sufficient for convenience at least, if*** not for speculative accuracy. If we suppose this extent to be something about one thousand miles each way, without, however, affecting much rigour in the limitation, the claim of New Holland to be called a continent, will be indisputable: The greatest extent of that vast country being, from East to West, about two thousand four hundred English miles, and, from North to South, not less than two thousand three hundred.****

[* Insula, from which island is derived, is formed from in sulo, in the sea; and, the corresponding word in Greek, is usually deduced from to swim, as appearing, and probably having been originally supposed to swim in the sea.]

[** Thus when Dionysius Periegetes considers the whole ancient world as surrounded by the sea, he calls it, an immense island; on which Eustathius remarks, that the addition of the epithet immense was necessary, otherwise the expression would have been low and inadequate.]

[*** We do not here consider whether a country be actually united under one government, but whether from its size it might be so conveniently. If we might derive from, or to inhabit, the etymological distinction would be complete on these principles. An island being one distinct habitation of men; and a continent land continued from one state to another. The former derivation might be rendered specious by remarking how singularly Homer and others use with, as if they had a natural connection. See II. B. 626. and, Sophoc. Ajax. 601.]

[**** In or near the latitude of 30° South, New Holland extends full 40 degrees of longitude, which, under that parallel, may be estimated at 60 English miles to a degree. The extent from York Cape to South Cape is full 33 degrees of latitude, which are calculated of course at 69½ English miles each.]

To New South Wales England has the claim which a tacit consent has generally made decisive among the European States, that of prior discovery. The whole of that Eastern coast, except the very Southern point, having been untouched by any navigator, till it was explored by Captain Cook. This consideration, added to the more favourable accounts given of this side of the continent than of the other, was sufficient to decide the choice of the British government, in appointing a place for the banishment of a certain class of criminals.

4

The cause of the determination to send out in this manner the convicts under sentence of transportation, was, as is well known, the necessary cessation of their removal to America; and the inconveniences experienced in the other modes of destination adopted after that period.

Virginia, greatly in want, at its first settlement, of labourers to clear away the impenetrable forests which impeded all cultivation, was willing, from very early times, to receive as servants, those English criminals whom our Courts of Law deemed not sufficiently guilty for capital punishment.* The planters hired their services during a limited term; and they were latterly sent out under the care of contractors, who were obliged to prove, by certificates, that they had disposed of them, according to the intention of the law.

[* Banishment was first ordered as a punishment for rogues and vagrants, by statute 39 Eliz. ch. 4. See Blackst. Com. IV. chap. 31. But no place was there specified. The practice of transporting criminals to America is said to have commenced in the reign of James I; the year 1619 being the memorable epoch of its origin: but that destination is first expressly mentioned in 18 Car. II. ch. 2.--The transport traffic was first regulated by statute 4 George I. ch. II. and the causes expressed in the preamble to be, the failure of those who undertook to transport themselves, and the great want of servants in his Majesty's plantations. Subsequent Acts enforced further regulations.]

The benefits of this regulation were various. The colonies received by it, at an easy rate, an assistance very necessary; and the mother country was relieved from the burthen of subjects, who at home were not only useless but pernicious: besides which, the mercantile returns, on this account alone, are reported to have arisen, in latter times, to a very considerable amount.* The individuals themselves, doubtless, in some instances, proved incorrigible; but it happened also, not very unfrequently, that, during the period of their legal servitude, they became reconciled to a life of honest industry, were altogether reformed in their manners, and rising gradually by laudable efforts, to situations of advantage, independence, and estimation, contributed honourably to the population and prosperity of their new country.**

[* It is said, forty thousand pounds per annum, about two thousand convicts being sold for twenty pounds each.]

[** The Abbe Raynal has given his full testimony to the policy of this species of banishment, in the fourteenth Book of his History, near the beginning.]

By the contest in America, and the subsequent separation of the thirteen Colonies, this traffic was of course destroyed. Other expedients, well known to the public, have since been tried; some of which proved highly objectionable;* and all have been found to want some of the principal advantages experienced from the usual mode of transportation.--The deliberations upon this subject, which more than once employed the attention of Parliament, produced at length the plan of which this volume displays the first result. On December 6, 1786, the proper orders were issued by his Majesty in Council, and an Act establishing a Court of Judicature in the place of settlement, and making such other regulations as the occasion required, received the sanction of the whole legislature early in the year 1787.

[* Particularly, the transporting of criminals to the coast of Africa, where what was meant as an alleviation of punishment too frequently ended in death.]

To expatiate upon the principles of penal law is foreign to the purpose of this work, but thus much is evident to the plainest apprehension, that the objects most to be desired in it are the restriction of the number of capital inflictions, as far as is consistent with the security of society; and the employment of every method that can be devised for rendering the guilty persons serviceable to the public, and just to themselves; for correcting their moral depravity, inducing habits of industry, and arming them in future against the temptations by which they have been once ensnared.

For effectuating these beneficial purposes, well regulated penitentiary houses seem, in speculation, to afford the fairest opportunity; and a plan of this kind, formed by the united efforts of Judge Blackstone, Mr. Eden, and Mr. Howard, was adopted by Parliament in the year 1779. Difficulties however occurred which prevented the execution of this design: a circumstance which will be something the less regretted when it shall be considered, that it is perhaps the fate of this theory, in common with many others of a very pleasing nature, to be more attractive in contemplation than efficacious in real practice. A perfect design, carried on by imperfect agents, is liable to lose the chief part of its excellence; and the best digested plan of confinement must in execution be committed, chiefly, to men not much enlightened, very little armed against corruption, and constantly exposed to the danger of it. The vigilance which in the infancy of such institutions effectually watches over the conduct of these public servants, will always in a little time be relaxed; and it will readily be conceived that a large penitentiary house, very corruptly governed, would be, of all associations, one of the most pernicious to those confined, and most dangerous to the peace of society.

In some countries, malefactors not capitally convicted, are sentenced to the gallies or the mines; punishments often more cruel than death, and here, on many accounts, impracticable. In other places they are employed in public works, under the care of overseers. This method has been partially tried in England on the Thames, but has been found by no means to produce the benefits expected from it. There is, therefore, little temptation to pursue it to a further extent. The employment of criminals in works carried on under the public eye, is perhaps too repugnant to the feelings of Englishmen ever to be tolerated. Reason, indeed, acquiesces in the melancholy necessity of punishing, but chains and badges of servitude are unpleasing objects, and compassion will always revolt at the sight of actual infliction. Convicts so employed would either by an ill placed charity be rewarded, or the people, undergoing a change of character far from desirable, would in time grow callous to those impressions which naturally impel them to give relief.

It remains therefore, that we adhere as much as possible to the practice approved by long experience, of employing the services of such criminals in remote and rising settlements. For this purpose the establishment on the eastern coast of New Holland has been projected, and carried on with every precaution to render it as beneficial as possible. That some difficulties will arise in the commencement of such an undertaking must be expected; but it is required by no moral obligation that convicts should be conveyed to a place of perfect convenience and security; and though the voluntary emigrants and honourable servants of the state, must in some measure, be involved for a time in the same disadvantages, yet to have resisted difficulties is often finally an advantage rather than an evil; and there are probably few persons so circumstanced who will repine at moderate hardships, when they reflect that by undergoing them they are rendering an essential and an honourable service to their country.

Chapter II.

March 1787 to June 1787

Preparation of the fleet ordered to Botany Bay.--Particulars of its arrangement.--Departure and passage to the Canary Isles.

16 March 1787

The squadron destined to carry into execution the above design, began to assemble at its appointed rendezvous, the Mother Bank, within the Isle of Wight, about the 16th of March, 1787. This small fleet consisted of the following ships: His Majesty's frigate *Sirius*, Captain John Hunter, and his Majesty's armed tender *Supply*, commanded by Lieutenant H. L. Ball. Three store-ships, the *Golden Grove*, *Fishburn*, and *Borrowdale*, for carrying provisions and stores for two years; including instruments of husbandry, clothing for the troops and convicts, and other necessaries; and lastly, six transports, the *Scarborough*, and *Lady Penrhyn*, from Portsmouth; the *Friendship*, and *Charlotte*, from Plymouth; the *Prince of Wales*, and the *Alexander*, from Woolwich. These were to carry the convicts, with a detachment of Marines in each, proportioned to the nature of the service; the largest where resistance was most to be expected, namely, in those ships which carried the greatest number of male convicts. Altogether they formed a little squadron of eleven sail.

They only who know the nature of such equipments, and consider the particular necessity in the present instance for a variety of articles not usually provided, can judge properly of the time required for furnishing out this fleet. Such persons will doubtless be the least surprised at being told that nearly two months had elapsed before the ships were enabled to quit this station, and proceed upon their voyage: and that even then some few articles were either unprepared, or, through misapprehension, neglected. The former circumstance took place respecting some part of the cloathing for the female convicts, which, being unfinished, was obliged to be left behind; the latter, with respect to the ammunition of the marines, which was furnished only for immediate service, instead of being, as the Commodore apprehended, completed at their first embarkation: an omission which, in the course of the voyage, was easily supplied.

This necessary interval was very usefully employed, in making the convicts fully sensible of the nature of their situation; in pointing out to them the advantages they would derive from good conduct, and the certainty of severe and immediate punishment in case of turbulence or mutiny. Useful regulations were at the same time established for the effectual governing of these people; and such measures were taken as could not fail to render abortive any plan they might be desperate enough to form for resisting authority, seizing any of the transports, or effecting, at any favourable period, an escape. We have, however, the testimony of those who commanded, that their behaviour, while the ships remained in port, was regular, humble, and in all respects suitable to their situation: such as could excite neither suspicion nor alarm, nor require the exertion of any kind of severity.

When the fleet was at length prepared for sailing, the complement of convicts and marines on board the transports was thus arranged. The *Friendship* carried a Captain and forty-four marines, subalterns and privates, with seventy-seven male and twenty female convicts. The *Charlotte*, a Captain and forty-three men, with eighty-eight male and twenty female convicts. In the *Alexander*, were two Lieutenants and thirty-five marines, with two hundred and thirteen convicts, all male. In the *Scarborough*, a Captain and thirty-three marines, with male convicts only, two hundred and eight in number. The *Prince of Wales* transport had two Lieutenants and thirty marines, with an hundred convicts, all female. And the *Lady Penrhyn*, a Captain, two Lieutenants, and only three privates, with one hundred and two female convicts. Ten marines, of different denominations, were also sent as supernumeraries on board the *Sirius*. The whole complement of marines, including officers, amounted to two hundred and twelve; besides which, twenty-eight women, wives of marines, carrying with them seventeen children, were permitted to accompany their husbands. The number of convicts was seven hundred and seventy-eight, of whom five hundred and fifty-eight were men. Two, however, on board the *Alexander*, received a full pardon before the departure of the fleet, and consequently remained in England.

13 May 1787

Governor Phillip, on his arrival at the station, hoisted his flag on board the *Sirius*, as Commodore of the squadron: and the embarkation being completed, and the time requiring his departure, at day break on the 13th of May, he gave the signal to weigh anchor. To the distance of about an hundred leagues clear of the channel, his Majesty's frigate Hyena, of twenty-four guns, was ordered to attend the fleet, in order to bring intelligence of its passage through that most difficult part of the voyage; with any dispatches which it might be requisite for the Governor to send home.

20 May 1787

On the 20th of May, the ships being then in latitude 47° 57', and longitude 12° 14' west of London, the Hyena returned. She brought, however, no exact account of the state of the transports; for the sea at that time ran so high, that the Governor found it difficult even to sit to write, and quite impracticable to send on board the several ships for exact reports of their situation, and of the behaviour of the convicts. All, however, had not been perfectly tranquil; the convicts in the *Scarborough*, confiding probably in their numbers, had formed a plan for gaining possession of that ship, which the officers had happily detected and frustrated. This information was received from them just before the Hyena sailed, and the Governor had ordered two of the ringleaders on board the *Sirius* for punishment. These men, after receiving a proper chastisement, were separated from their party by being removed into another ship, the *Prince of Wales*. No other attempt of this kind was made during the voyage.

We may now consider the adventurers in this small fleet as finally detached, for the present, from their native country; looking forward, doubtless with very various emotions, to that unknown region, which, for a time at least, they were destined to inhabit. If we would indulge a speculative curiosity, concerning the tendency of such an enterprize, there are few topics which would afford an ampler scope for conjecture. The sanguine might form expectations of extraordinary consequences, and be justified, in some degree, by the reflection, that from smaller, and not more respectable beginnings, powerful empires have frequently arisen. The phlegmatic and apprehensive might magnify to themselves the difficulties of the undertaking, and prognosticate, from various causes, the total failure of it. Both, perhaps, would be wrong. The opinion nearest to the right was probably formed by the Governor himself, and such others among the leaders of the expedition, as from native courage, felt themselves superior to all difficulties likely to occur; and by native good sense were secured from the seduction of romantic reveries. To all it must appear a striking proof of the flourishing state of navigation in the present age, and a singular illustration of its vast progress since the early nautical efforts of mankind; that whereas the ancients coasted with timidity along the shores of the Mediterranean, and thought it a great effort to run across the narrow sea which separates Crete from Egypt, Great Britain, without hesitation, sends out a fleet to plant a settlement near the antipodes.

3 June 1787

The high sea which had impeded the intercourse between the ships, as they were out of the reach of rocks and shoals, was not, in other respects, an unfavourable circumstance. On the whole, therefore, the weather was reckoned fine, and the passage very prosperous from Spithead to Santa Cruz, in the Isle of Teneriffe, where the fleet anchored on the 3d of June.

Chapter III.

June 1787

Reasons for touching at the Canary Isles--Precautions for preserving Health--Their admirable Success--Some Account of the Canaries--Fables respecting them--Attempt of a Convict to escape--Departure.

3 June 1787

The chief object proposed by Governor Phillip in touching at Teneriffe, was the obtaining a fresh supply of water and vegetables. It was adviseable also at this period to give the people such advantages and refreshments, for the sake of health, as this place would readily supply, but which can only be obtained on shore. In this, and every port, the crews, soldiers, and convicts, were indulged with fresh meat, fruit, vegetables, and every thing which could conduce to preserve them from the complaints formerly inevitable in long voyages. The allowance was, to the marines, a pound of bread, a pound of beef, and a pint of wine per man, daily: the convicts had three quarters of a pound of beef, and of bread, but no wine. The fruits obtained here were only figs and mulberries, but these were plentiful and excellent. How successfully precautions of every kind, tending to this great end, were employed throughout the voyage, the reports of the number of sick and dead will sufficiently evince.

Captain Cook had very fully shown, how favourable such expeditions might be made to the health of those engaged in them; and Governor Phillip was happy enough to confirm the opinion, that the success of his great predecessor, in this essential point, was not in any degree the effect of chance, but arose from that care and attention of which he has humanely given us the detail; and which, in similar circumstances, may generally be expected to produce the same result. If the number of convicts who died between the time of embarkation and the arrival of the fleet at this place, should seem inconsistent with this assertion, it must be considered that the deaths were confined entirely to that class of people, many of whom were advanced in years, or labouring under diseases contracted in prison or elsewhere, while they were yet on shore.

A week was passed at this place, during which time the weather was very moderate, the thermometer not exceeding 70° of Fahrenheit's scale. The barometer stood at about 30 inches.

The Governor of the Canaries, at this time, was the Marquis de Brancifort, by birth a Sicilian. He was resident as usual at Santa Cruz, and paid to Governor Phillip, and the other officers, a polite attention and respect equally honourable to all parties. The port of Santa Cruz, though not remarkably fine, is yet the best in the Canaries, and the usual place at which vessels touch for refreshment; the residence of the Governor General is therefore fixed always in Teneriffe, for the sake of a more frequent intercourse with Europe: in preference to the great Canary Isle, which contains the Metropolitan church, and the palace of the Bishop. The Marquis de Brancifort has lately established some useful manufactures in Teneriffe.

To enter into much detail concerning the Canary Islands, which lie exactly in the course of every ship that sails from Europe to the Cape, and consequently have been described in almost every book of voyages, must be superfluous. A few general notices concerning them may, perhaps, not be unacceptable. They are in number about fourteen, of which the principal, and only considerable are, Canary, Teneriffe, Fortaventure, Palma, Ferro, Gomera, Lancerotta. Their distance from the coast of Africa is from about forty to eighty leagues. The circumference of Teneriffe is not above one hundred and twenty miles, but that of Canary, or as it is usually called, the Great Canary, is one hundred and fifty. They have been possessed and colonized by Spain from the beginning of the 15th century.

There is no reason to doubt that these are the islands slightly known to the ancients under the name of Fortunate: though the mistake of Ptolemy concerning their latitude has led one of the commentators on Solinus to contend, that this title belongs rather to the Islands of Cape Verd. Pliny mentions Canaria, and accounts for that name from the number of large dogs which the island contained; a circumstance which some modern voyagers, perhaps with little accuracy, repeat as having occasioned the same name to be given by the Spaniards. Nivaria, spoken of by the same author, is evidently Teneriffe, and synonymous, if we are rightly informed, to the modern name*. Ombrion, or Pluvialia, is supposed to be Ferro; where the dryness of the soil has at all times compelled the inhabitants to depend for water on the rains.

[* Occasioned by the perpetual snows with which the Peak is covered. Tener is said to mean snow, and itte or iffe a mountain, in the language of the island.]

If the ancients made these islands the region of fable, and their poets decorated them with imaginary charms to supply the want of real knowledge, the moderns cannot wholly be exempted from a similar imputation. Travellers have delighted to speak of the Peak of Teneriffe, as the highest mountain in the ancient world, whereas, by the best accounts, Mont Blanc exceeds it* by 3523 feet, or near a mile of perpendicular altitude. The Isle of Ferro, having no such mountain to distinguish it, was celebrated for a century or two on the credit of a miraculous tree, single in its kind, enveloped in perpetual mists, and distilling sufficient water for the ample supply of the island.** But this wonder, though vouched by several voyagers, and by some as eye-witnesses, vanished at the approach of sober enquiry, nor could a single native be found hardy enough to assert its existence. The truth is, that the Canary Isles, though a valuable possession to Spain, and an excellent resource to voyagers of all nations, contain no wonders, except what belong naturally to volcanic mountains such as the Peak, which, though it always threatens, has not now been noxious for more than eighty years***.

[* The height of Mont Blanc, on a mean of the best accounts, is 15,673 English feet from the level of the sea, Teneriffe 12,150.]

[** Clipperton speaks of it as a fact, Harris's Voyages, Vol. I. p. 187. Mandelsloe pretended to have seen it, ibid. p. 806. Baudrand was the first who by careful enquiry detected the fiction. An account of this imaginary tree, curious from being so circumstantial, is here given from a French book of geography, of some credit in other respects. "Mais ce qu'il-y-a de plus digne de remarque, est cet arbre merveilleux qui fournit d'eau toute l'isle, tant pour les hommes que pour les bêtes. Cet arbre, que les habitans appellent Caroë, Garoë, ou Arbre Saint, unique en son espéce, est gros, et large de branches; son tronc a environ douze pieds de tour; ses feuilles sont un peu plus grosses que celles des noiers, et toujours vertes; il porte un fruit, semblable à un gland, qui a un noiau d'un goût aromatique, doux et piquant. Cet arbre est perpétuellement convert d'un nuage, qui l'humecte partout, en sorte que l'eau en distille goutte à goutte par les branches et par les feuilles, en telle quantité qu'on en peut emplir trente tonneaux par jour. Cette eau est extrémement fraiche, claire, fort bonne a boire, et fort saine. Elle tombe dans deux bassins de pierre que les insulaires ont bâtis pour la recevoir. La nuage qui couvre cet arbre ne se dissipe pas; settlement dans les grandes chaleurs de l'été il se diminue un peu; mais en échange la mer envoie une vapeur epaisse, qui se jette sur l'arbre, et qui supplée a ce manquement." Du Bois Geogr. Part. iii. ch. 17. Can all this have arisen from Pliny's arbores ex quibus aquae exprimantur?]

[*** See Captain Glasse's elaborate account of the Canaries, and Captain Cook's last Voyage.]

The capital of Teneriffe is Laguna, or more properly San Christoval de la Laguna, St. Christopher of the Lake, so called from its situation near a lake. Both this and Santa Cruz are built of stone, but the appearance of the latter is more pleasing than that of Laguna. They are distant from each other about four miles. The capital of the Great Canary, and properly of the whole government, is the City of Palms: But that place has been for some time the centre of ecclesiastical government only. The custom of reckoning the first meridian as passing through these isles was begun by Ptolemy; and perhaps it is still to be wished that the French regulations on that subject were generally adopted.

9 June 1787.

Our ships were at length preparing to depart, when on the evening of the 9th of June, a convict belonging to the *Alexander*, having been employed on deck, found means to cut away the boat, and make a temporary escape; but he was missed and soon retaken. It is not probable that he had formed any definite plan of escape; the means of absconding must have been accidentally offered, and suddenly embraced; and for making such an attempt, the vague hope of liberty, without any certain prospect, would naturally afford sufficient temptation.

10 June 1787

By the 10th of June the ships had completed their water, and early the next morning, the Governor gave the signal for weighing anchor, and the fleet pursued its course.

Report of the marines and convicts under medical treatment, given in to Governor Phillip, June 4th, 1787.

Charlotte, -- Marines 4 Convicts 16 *Alexander*, -- Marines 2 Convicts 26*Scarborough*, -- Marine 1 Convicts 9 *Friendship*, -- Convicts 13 *Lady Penrhyn*, Convicts 11 *Prince of Wales*, Marines 2 Convicts 7 --- Total Marines 9 Convicts 72

Convicts dead since the first embarkation 21 Children of convicts 3

Of these only fifteen, and one child, had died since the departure from Spithead.

Chapter IV.

June 1787 to September 1787

Attempt to put in at Port Praya--Relinquished--Weather--Sail for Rio de Faneiro--Reasons for touching at a South American port--The Fleet passes the Line--Arrives at Rio de Faneiro--Account of that Place--Transactions there--Departure.

Vegetables not having been so plentiful at Santa Cruz as to afford a sufficient supply, it was the intention of Governor Phillip to anchor for about twenty-four hours in the Bay of Port Praya. The islands on this side of the Atlantic, seem as if expressly placed to facilitate the navigation to and from the Cape of Good Hope: by offering to vessels, without any material variation from their course, admirable stations for supply and refreshment. About latitude 40, north, the Azores; in 33, the Madeiras; between 29 and 27, the Canaries; and between 18 and 16, the Islands of Cape Verd, successively offer themselves to the voyager, affording abundantly every species of accommodation his circumstances can require. On the Southern side of the Equator, a good harbour and abundance of turtles give some consequence even to the little

9

barren island of Ascension; and St. Helena, by the industry of the English settlers, has become the seat of plenty and of elegance. Without the assistance derived, in going or returning, from some of these places, the interval of near forty degrees on each side of the line, in a sea exposed to violent heat, and subject to tedious calms, would be sufficient to discourage even the navigators of the eighteenth century.

18 June 1787

On the 18th of June, the fleet came in sight of the Cape Verd Islands, and was directed by signal to steer for St. Jago. But the want of favourable wind, and the opposition of a strong current making it probable that all the ships would not be able to get into the Bay, the Governor thought it best to change his plan. The signal for anchoring was hauled down, and the ships were directed to continue their first course; a circumstance of much disappointment to many individuals on board, who, as is natural in long voyages, were eager on every occasion to enjoy the refreshments of the shore. As an additional incitement to such wishes, the weather had now become hot; the thermometer stood at 82°, which, though not an immoderate heat for a tropical climate, is sufficient to produce considerable annoyance. But, unmoved by any consideration except that of expedience, Governor Phillip persisted in conducting his ships to their next intended station, the harbour of Rio de Janeiro.

It may appear perhaps, on a slight consideration, rather extraordinary, that vessels bound to the Cape of Good Hope should find it expedient to touch at a harbour of South America. To run across the Atlantic, and take as a part of their course, that coast, the very existence of which was unknown to the first navigators of these seas, seems a very circuitous method of performing the voyage. A little examination will remove this apparent difficulty. The calms so frequent on the African side, are of themselves a sufficient cause to induce a navigator to keep a very westerly course; and even the islands at which it is so often convenient to touch will carry him within a few degrees of the South American coast.--The returning tracks of Captain Cooks's three voyages all run within a very small space of the 45th degree of west longitude, which is even ten degrees further to the west than the extremity of Cape St. Roque: and that course appears to have been taken voluntarily, without any extraordinary inducement. But in the latitudes to which Governor Phillip's squadron had now arrived, the old and new continent approach so near to each other, that in avoiding the one it becomes necessary to run within a very moderate distance of the opposite land.

In the passage from the Cape Verd Islands, the fleet suffered for some time the inconvenience of great heat, attended by heavy rains. The heat, however, did not at any time exceed the point already specified,* and the precautions unremittingly observed in all the ships happily continued efficacious in preventing any violent sickness. Nor did the oppression of the hot weather continue so long as in these latitudes might have been expected; for before they reached the equator the temperature had become much more moderate.

[* 82°, 51. It is not unusual in England, to have the thermometer, for a day or two in a summer, at 81°.]

5 July 1787

On July 5, 1787, being then in long. 26° 10' west from Greenwich, the Botany Bay fleet passed from the Northern into the Southern Hemisphere. About three weeks more of very favourable and pleasant weather conveyed them to Rio de Janeiro.

5-6 August 1787

On the 5th of August they anchored off the harbour, and on the evening of the 6th were at their station within it. The land of Cape Frio had been discovered some days before, but a deficiency of wind from that time a little slackened their course.

Rio de Janeiro, or January River, so called because discovered by Dias de Solis on the feast of St. Januarius, (Sept. 19) 1525, is not in fact a river, though its name denotes that it was then supposed to be so: it is an arm of the sea, into which a considerable number of small rivers descends.

The city of Rio de Janeiro, called by some writers St. Sebastian, from the name of its tutelar patron, is situated on the west side of this bay, within less than a degree of the tropic of Capricorn, and about 43° west of Greenwich. It is at present the capital of all Brasil, and has been for some time the residence of the Viceroy. These distinctions it obtained in preference to St. Salvador, which was formerly the capital, by means of the diamond mines discovered in its vicinity, in the year 1730. The place increasing rapidly by the wealth thus brought to it, was fortified and put under the care of a governor in 1738. The port is one of the finest in the world, very narrow at the entrance, and within capacious enough to contain more ships than ever were assembled at one station. It has soundings from twenty to one hundred and twenty fathoms. A hill shaped like a sugar loaf, situated on the west side, marks the proper bearing for entering the harbour: the situation of which is fully pointed out at the distance of two leagues and a half by some small islands, one of which, called Rodonda, is very high, and in form not unlike a haycock. The mouth of the harbour is defended by forts, particularly two, called Santa Cruz and Lozia; and the usual anchorage within it is before the city, north of a small island named Dos Cobras.

There are in this port established fees, which are paid by all merchant ships, Portuguese as well as strangers: 3l. 12s. each on entering the bay, the same on going out, and 5s. 6d. a day while they remain at anchor. The entrance fee was demanded for the transports in this expedition, but when Governor Phillip had alledged that they were loaded with King's stores, the payment was no more insisted upon. Nevertheless, the Captain of the Port gave his attendance, with his boat's crew, to assist the ships in coming in, there being at that time only a light air, hardly sufficient to carry them up the bay.

In the narrative of Captain Cook's Voyage in 1768, we find, on his arrival at this place, great appearance of suspicion on the part of the Viceroy, harsh prohibitions of landing, even to the gentlemen employed in philosophical researches, and some proceedings rather of a violent nature. The reception given by the present Viceroy to Governor Phillip and his officers was very different: it was polite and flattering to a great degree, and free from every tincture of jealous caution.

Don Lewis de Varconcellos, the reigning Viceroy, belongs to one of the noblest families in Portugal; is brother to the Marquis of Castello Methor, and to the Count of Pombeiro. Governor Phillip, who served for some years as a Captain in the Portuguese navy, and is deservedly much honoured by that nation, was not personally unknown to the Viceroy, though known in a way which, in a less liberal mind, might have produced very different dispositions. There had been some difference between them, on a public account, in this port, when Governor Phillip commanded the Europe: each party had acted merely for the honour of the nation to which he belonged, and the Viceroy, with the true spirit of a man of honour, far from resenting a conduct so similar to his own, seemed now to make it his object to obliterate every recollection of offence. As soon as he was fully informed of the nature of Governor Phillip's commission, he gave it out in orders to the garrison that the same honours should be paid to that officer as to himself. This distinction the Governor modestly wished to decline, but was not permitted. His officers were all introduced to the Viceroy, and were, as well as himself, received with every possible mark of attention to them, and regard for their country. They were allowed to visit all parts of the city, and even to make excursions as far as five miles into the country, entirely unattended: an indulgence very unusual to strangers, and considering what we read of the jealousy of the Portuguese Government respecting its diamond mines, the more extraordinary.

Provisions were here so cheap, that notwithstanding the allowance of meat was fixed by Governor Phillip at twenty ounces a day, the men were victualled completely, rice, fresh vegetables, and firing included, at three-pence three-farthings a head. Wine was not at this season to be had, except from the retail dealers, less was therefore purchased than would otherwise have been taken. Rum, however, was laid in; and all such seeds and plants procured as were thought likely to flourish on the coast of New South Wales, particularly coffee, indigo, cotton, and the cochineal fig.* As a substitute for bread, if it should become scarce, one hundred sacks of cassada were purchased at a very advantageous price.

[* Cactus Cochinilifer, of Linnaeus.]

Cassada, the bread of thousands in the tropical climates, affords one of those instances in which the ingenuity of man might be said to triumph over the intentions of nature, were it not evidently the design of Providence that we should in all ways exert our invention and sagacity to the utmost, for our own security and support. It is the root of a shrub called Cassada, or Cassava Jatropha, and in its crude state is highly poisonous. By washing, pressure, and evaporation, it is deprived of all its noxious qualities, and being formed into cakes becomes a salubrious and not an unpalatable substitute for bread.

By the indulgence of the Viceroy, the deficiency in the military stores observed at the departure of the transports from England, was made up by a supply purchased from the Royal arsenal; nor was any assistance withheld which either the place afforded, or the stores of government could furnish.

The circumstances, which in this place most astonish a stranger, and particularly a Protestant, are, the great abundance of images dispersed throughout the city, and the devotion paid to them. They are placed at the corner of almost every street, and are never passed without a respectful salutation; but at night they are constantly surrounded by their respective votaries, who offer up their prayers aloud, and make the air resound in all quarters with the notes of their hymns. The strictness of manners in the inhabitants is not said to be at all equivalent to the warmth of this devotion; but in all countries and climates it is found much easier to perform external acts of reputed piety, than to acquire the internal habits so much more essential. It must be owned, however, that our people did not find the ladies so indulgent as some voyagers have represented them.

It was near a month before Governor Phillip could furnish his ships with every thing which it was necessary they should now procure. At length, on the 4th of September he weighed anchor, and as he passed the fort, received from the Viceroy the last compliment it was in his power to pay, being saluted with twenty-one guns. The salute was returned by an equal number from the *Sirius*; and thus ended an intercourse honourable to both nations, and particularly to the principal officer employed in the service of each.

Chapter V.

September 1787 to January 1788

Prospercus passage from Rio to the Cape--Account of the Harbours there--The Cape of Good Hope not the most Southern point--Height of Table Mountain and others--Supineness of the European nations in neglecting to occupy the Cape--Live stock laid in--Departure--Separation of the fleet--Arrival of the *Supply* at Botany Bay.

4 September 1787

A Prosperous course by sea, like a state of profound peace and tranquility in civil society, though most advantageous to those who enjoy it, is unfavourable to the purposes of narration. The striking facts which the writer exerts himself to record, and the reader is eager to peruse, arise only from difficult situations: uniform prosperity is described in very few words. Of this acceptable but unproductive kind was the passage of the Botany Bay fleet from Rio de Janeiro to the Cape of Good Hope; uniformly favourable, and not marked by any extraordinary incidents. This run, from about lat. 22° south, long. 43 west of London, to lat. 34° south, long. 18° east of London, a distance of about four thousand miles, was performed in thirty-nine days: for having left Rio on the 4th of September, on the 13th of October the ships came to anchor in Table Bay. Here they were to take their final refreshment, and lay in every kind of stock with which they were not already provided. In this period no additional lives had been lost, except that of a single convict belonging to the *Charlotte* transport, who fell accidentally into the sea, and could not by any efforts be recovered.

13 October 1787

Table Bay, on the north-west side of the Cape of Good Hope, is named from the Table Mountain, a promontory of considerable elevation, at the foot of which, and almost in the centre of the Bay, stands Cape Town, the principal Dutch settlement in this territory. This Bay cannot properly be called a port, being by no means a station of security; it is exposed to all the violence of the winds which set into it from the sea; and is far from sufficiently secured from those which blow from the land. The gusts which descend from the summit of Table Mountain are sufficient to force ships from their anchors, and even violently to annoy persons on the shore, by destroying any tents or other temporary edifices which may be erected, and raising clouds of fine dust, which produce very troublesome effects. A gale of this kind, from the south-east, blew for three days successively when Capt. Cook lay here in his first voyage, at which time, he informs us, the Resolution was the only ship in the harbour that had not dragged her anchors. The storms from the sea are still more formidable; so much so, that ships have frequently been driven by them from their anchorage, and wrecked at the head of the Bay. But these accidents happen chiefly in the quaade mousson, or winter months, from May 14 to the same day of August; during which time few ships venture to anchor here. Our fleet, arriving later, lay perfectly unmolested as long as it was necessary for it to remain in this station.

False Bay, on the south-east side of the Cape, is more secure than Table Bay, during the prevalence of the north-west winds, but still less so in strong gales from the south-east. It is however less frequented, being twenty-four miles of very heavy road distant from Cape Town, whence almost all necessaries must be procured. The most sheltered part of False Bay is a recess on the west side, called Simon's Bay.

The Cape of Good Hope, though popularly called, and perhaps pretty generally esteemed so, is not in truth the most southern point of Africa. The land which projects furthest to the south is a point to the east of it, called by the English Cape Lagullus; a name corrupted from the original Portugueze das Agulhas, which, as well as the French appellation des Aiguilles, is descriptive of its form, and would rightly be translated Needle Cape. Three eminences, divided by very narrow passes, and appearing in a distant view like three summits of the same mountain, stand at the head of Table Bay.--They are however of different heights, by which difference, as well as by that of their shape, they may be distinguished. Table Mountain is so called from its appearance, as it terminates in a flat horizontal surface, from which the face of the rock descends almost perpendicularly. This mountain rises to about 3567 feet above the level of the sea. Devil's Head, called also Charles mountain, is situated to the east of the former, and is not above 3368 feet in height; and on the west side of Table Mountain, Lion's Head, whose name is also meant to be descriptive, does not exceed 2764 feet. In the neighbourhood of the latter lies Constantia, a district consisting of two farms, wherein the famous wines of that name are produced.

Our voyagers found provisions less plentiful and less reasonable in price at Cape Town than they had been taught to expect. Board and lodging, which are to be had only in private houses, stood the officers in two rix-dollars a day, which is near nine shillings sterling. This town, the only place in the whole colony to which that title can be applied with propriety, is of no great extent; it does not in any part exceed two miles: and the country, colonized here by the Dutch, is in general so unfavourable to cultivation, that it is not without some astonishment that we find them able to raise provisions from it in sufficient abundance to supply themselves, and the ships of so many nations which constantly resort to the Cape.

When we consider the vast advantages derived by the Dutch colonists from this traffic, and the almost indispensible necessity by which navigators of all nations are driven to seek refreshment there, it cannot but appear extraordinary, that from the discovery of the Cape in 1493, by Barthelemi Diaz, to the year 1650, when, at the suggestion of John Van Riebeck, the first Dutch colony was sent, a spot so very favourable to commerce and navigation should have remained unoccupied by Europeans. Perhaps all the perseverance of the Dutch character was necessary even to suggest the idea of maintaining an establishment in a soil so burnt by the sun, and so little disposed to repay the toil of the cultivator. The example and success of this people may serve, however, as an useful instruction to all who in great undertakings are deterred by trifling obstacles; and who, rather than contend with difficulties, are inclined to relinquish the most evident advantages.

But though the country near the Cape had not charms enough to render it as pleasing as that which surrounds Rio de Janeiro, yet the Governor, Mynheer Van Graaffe, was not far behind the Viceroy of Brazil in attention to the English officers. They were admitted to his table, where they were elegantly entertained, and had reason to be pleased in all respects with his behaviour and disposition. Yet the minds of his people were not at this time in a tranquil state; the accounts from Holland were such as occasioned much uneasiness, and great preparations were making at the fort, from apprehension of a rupture with some other power.

In the course of a month, the live stock and other provisions were procured; and the ships, having on board not less than five hundred animals of different kinds, but chiefly poultry, put on an appearance which naturally enough excited the idea of Noah's ark. This supply, considering that the country had previously suffered from a dearth, was very considerable; but it was purchased of course at a higher expence considerably than it would have been in a time of greater plenty.

12 November 1787

On the 12th of November the fleet set sail, and was for many days much delayed by strong winds from the south-east.

25 November 1787

On the 25th, being then only 80 leagues to the eastward of the Cape, Governor Phillip left the *Sirius* and went on board the *Supply* tender; in hopes, by leaving the convoy, to gain sufficient time for examining the country round Botany Bay, so as to fix on the situation most eligible for the colony, before the transports should arrive. At the same time he ordered the agents for the transports, who were in the *Alexander*, to separate themselves from the convoy with that ship, the *Scarborough* and *Friendship*, which, as they were better sailors than the rest, might reasonably be expected sooner: in which case, by the labour of the convicts they had on board, much might be done in making the necessary preparations for landing the provisions and stores.

Major Ross, the Commandant of Marines, now left the *Sirius*, and went on board the *Scarborough*, that he might accompany that part of the detachment which probably would be landed first. Captain Hunter, in the *Sirius*, was to follow with the store-ships, and the remainder of the transports; and he had the necessary instructions for his future proceedings, in case the *Supply* had met with any accident. Lieutenant Gidley King, since appointed Commandant of Norfolk Island, accompanied Governor Phillip in the *Supply*.

3 January 1788

From this time to the 3d of January, 1788, the winds were as favourable as could be wished, blowing generally in very strong gales from the north-west, west, and south-west. Once only the wind had shifted to the east, but continued in that direction not more than a few hours. Thus assisted, the *Supply*, which sailed but very indifferently, and turned out, from what she had suffered in the voyage, to be hardly a safe conveyance, performed in fifty-one days a voyage of more than seven thousand miles. On the day abovementioned she was within sight of the coast of New South Wales. But the winds then became variable, and a current, which at times set very strongly to the southward, so much impeded her course, that it was not till the 18th that she arrived at Botany Bay.

13

Chapter VI.

January 1788

First interview with the natives--the bay examined--arrival of the whole fleet--Port Jackson examined--second interview with the natives--and third--Governor Phillip returns to Botany Bay--and gives orders for the evacuation of it.

18 January 1788

At the very first landing of Governor Phillip on the shore of Botany Bay, an interview with the natives took place. They were all armed, but on seeing the Governor approach with signs of friendship, alone and unarmed, they readily returned his confidence by laying down their weapons. They were perfectly devoid of cloathing, yet seemed fond of ornaments, putting the beads and red baize that were given them, on their heads or necks, and appearing pleased to wear them. The presents offered by their new visitors were all readily accepted, nor did any kind of disagreement arise while the ships remained in Botany Bay. This very pleasing effect was produced in no small degree by the personal address, as well as by the great care and attention of the Governor. Nor were the orders which enforced a conduct so humane, more honourable to the persons from whom they originated, than the punctual execution of them was to the officers sent out: it was evident that their wishes coincided with their duty; and that a sanguinary temper was no longer to disgrace the European settlers in countries newly discovered.

The next care after landing was the examination of the bay itself, from which it appeared that, though extensive, it did not afford a shelter from the easterly winds: and that, in consequence of its shallowness, ships even of a moderate draught, would always be obliged to anchor with the entrance of the bay open, where they must be exposed to a heavy sea, that rolls in whenever it blows hard from the eastward.

Several runs of fresh water were found in different parts of the bay, but there did not appear to be any situation to which there was not some very strong objection. In the northern part of it is a small creek, which runs a considerable way into the country, but it has water only for a boat, the sides of it are frequently overflowed, and the low lands near it are a perfect swamp. The western branch of the bay is continued to a great extent, but the officers sent to examine it could not find there any supply of fresh water, except in very small drains.

Point Sutherland offered the most eligible situation, having a run of good water, though not in very great abundance. But to this part of the harbour the ships could not approach, and the ground near it, even in the higher parts, was in general damp and spungy. Smaller numbers might indeed in several spots have found a comfortable residence, but no place was found in the whole circuit of Botany Bay which seemed at all calculated for the reception of so large a settlement. While this examination was carried on, the whole fleet had arrived. The *Supply* had not so much outsailed the other ships as to give Governor Phillip the advantage he had expected in point of time. On the 19th of January, the *Alexander*, *Scarborough*, and *Friendship*, cast anchor in Botany Bay; and on the 20th, the *Sirius*, with the remainder of the convoy*. These ships had all continued very healthy; they had not, however, yet arrived at their final station.

[* The annexed view of Botany Bay, represents the *Supply*, etc. at anchor, and the *Sirius* with her convoy coming into the bay.]

A View of Botany Bay

The openness of this bay, and the dampness of the soil, by which the people would probably be rendered unhealthy, had already determined the Governor to seek another situation. He resolved, therefore, to examine Port Jackson, a bay mentioned by Captain Cook as immediately to the north of this. There he hoped to find, not only a better harbour, but a fitter place for the establishment of his new government. But that no time might be lost, in case of a disappointment in these particulars, the ground near Point Sutherland was ordered immediately to be cleared, and preparations to be made for landing, under the direction of the Lieutenant Governor.

These arrangements having been settled, Governor Phillip prepared to proceed to the examination of Port Jackson: and as the time of his absence, had he gone in the *Supply*, must have been very uncertain, he went round with three boats; taking with him Captain Hunter and several other officers, that by examining several parts of the harbour at once the greater dispatch might be made.

22d January, 1788.

On the 22d of January they set out upon this expedition, and early in the afternoon arrived at Port Jackson, which is distant about three leagues. Here all regret arising from the former disappointments was at once obliterated; and Governor Phillip had the satisfaction to find one of the finest harbours in the world, in which a thousand sail of the line might ride in perfect security.

The different coves of this harbour were examined with all possible expedition, and the preference was given to one which had the finest spring of water, and in which ships can anchor so close to the shore, that at a very small expence quays may be constructed at which the largest vessels may unload. This cove is about half a mile in length, and a quarter of a mile across at the entrance. In honour of Lord Sydney, the Governor distinguished it by the name of Sydney Cove.

On the arrival of the boats at Port Jackson, a second party of the natives made its appearance near the place of landing. These also were armed with lances, and at first were very vociferous; but the same gentle means used towards the others easily persuaded these also to discard their suspicions, and to accept whatsoever was offered. One man in particular, who appeared to be the chief of this tribe, shewed very singular marks both of confidence in his new friends, and of determined resolution. Under the guidance of Governor Phillip, to whom he voluntarily intrusted himself, he went to a part of the beach where the men belonging to the boats were then boiling their meat: when he approached the marines, who were drawn up near that place, and saw that by proceeding he should be separated from his companions, who remained with several of the officers at some distance, he stopped, and with great firmness, seemed by words and gestures to threaten revenge if any advantage should be taken of his situation. He then went on with perfect calmness to examine what was boiling in the pot, and by the manner in which he expressed his admiration, made it evident that he intended to profit by what he saw. Governor Phillip contrived to make him understand that large shells might conveniently be used for the same purpose, and it is probable that by these hints, added to his own observation, he will be enabled to introduce the art of boiling among his countrymen. Hitherto they appear to have known no other way of dressing food than broiling. Their methods of kindling fire are probably very imperfect and laborious, for it is observed that they usually keep it burning, and are very rarely seen without either a fire actually made, or a piece of lighted wood, which they carry with them from place to place, and even in their canoes.* The perpetual fires, which in some countries formed a part of the national religion, had perhaps no other origin than a similar inability to produce it at pleasure; and if we suppose the original flame to have been kindled by lightning, the fiction of its coming down from heaven will be found to deviate very little from the truth.

[* In Hawksw. Voy. vol. iii. p. 234, it is said that they produce fire with great facility, etc. which account is the more correct, time will probably show.]

In passing near a point of land in this harbour, the boats were perceived by a number of the natives, twenty of whom waded into the water unarmed, received what was offered them, and examined the boat with a curiosity which impressed a higher idea of them than any former accounts of their manners had suggested. This confidence, and manly behaviour, induced Governor Phillip, who was highly pleased with it, to give the place the name of Manly Cove. The same people afterwards joined the party at the place where they had landed to dine. They were then armed, two of them with shields and swords, the rest with lances only. The swords were made of wood, small in the gripe, and apparently less formidable than a good stick. One of these men had a kind of white clay rubbed upon the upper part of his face, so as to have the appearance of a mask. This ornament, if it can be called such, is not common among them, and is probably assumed only on particular occasions, or as a distinction to a few individuals. One woman had been seen on the rocks as the boats passed, with her face, neck and breasts thus painted, and to our people appeared the most disgusting figure imaginable; her own countrymen were perhaps delighted by the beauty of the effect.

During the preparation for dinner the curiosity of these visitors rendered them very troublesome, but an innocent contrivance altogether removed the inconvenience. Governor Phillip drew a circle round the place where the English were, and without much difficulty made the natives understand that they were not to pass that line; after which they sat down in perfect quietness. Another proof how tractable these people are, when no insult or injury is offered, and when proper means are to influence the simplicity of their minds.

24 January 1788

January 24th, 1788. On the 24th of January, Governor Phillip having sufficiently explored Port Jackson, and found it in all respects highly calculated to receive such a settlement as he was appointed to establish, returned to Botany Bay. On his arrival there, the reports made to him, both of the ground which the people were clearing, and of the upper parts of the Bay, which in this interval had been more particularly examined, were in the greatest degree unfavourable. It was impossible after this to hesitate concerning the choice of a situation; and orders were accordingly issued for the removal of the whole fleet to Port Jackson.

That Botany Bay should have appeared to Captain Cook in a more advantageous light than to Governor Phillip, is not by any means extraordinary. Their objects were very different; the one required only shelter and refreshment for a small vessel, and during but a short time: the other had great numbers to provide for, and was necessitated to find a place wherein ships of very considerable burthen might approach the shore with ease, and lie at all times in perfect security. The appearance of the place is picturesque and pleasing, and the ample harvest it afforded, of botanical acquisitions, made it interesting to the philosophical gentlemen engaged in that expedition; but something more essential than beauty of appearance, and more necessary than philosophical riches, must be sought in a place where the permanent residence of multitudes is to be established.

Chapter VII.

January 1788

Removal from Botany Bay--Arrival of two French ships--Account of them--Preparations for encampment--Difficulties--Scurvy breaks out--Account of the red and yellow gum trees.

24 January 1788

Preparations for a general removal were now made with all convenient expedition: but on the morning of the 24th the greatest astonishment was spread throughout the fleet by the appearance of two ships, under French colours. In this remote region visitors from Europe were very little expected, and their arrival, while the cause of it remained unknown, produced in some minds a temporary apprehension, accompanied by a multiplicity of conjectures, many of them sufficiently ridiculous. Governor Phillip was the first to recollect that two ships had been sent out some time before from France for the purpose of discovery, and rightly concluded these to be the same. But as the opposition of the wind, and a strong current prevented them at present from working into the harbour, and even drove them out of sight again to the south, he did not think proper to delay his departure for the sake of making further enquiry.

25 January 1788

On the 25th of January therefore, seven days after the arrival of the *Supply*, Governor Phillip quitted Botany Bay in the same ship, and sailed to Port Jackson. The rest of the fleet, under convoy of the *Sirius*, was ordered to follow, as soon as the abatement of the wind, which then blew a strong gale, should facilitate its working out of the Bay. The *Supply* was scarcely out of sight when the French ships again appeared off the mouth of the harbour, and a boat was immediately sent to them, with offers of every kind of information and assistance their situation could require. It was now learnt that these were, as the Governor had supposed, the *Boussole* and the *Astrolabe*, on a voyage of discovery, under the conduct of Monsieur La Perouse.

26 January 1788

On the 26th, the transports and store ships, attended by the *Sirius*, finally evacuated Botany Bay; and in a very short time they were all assembled in Sydney Cove, the place now destined for their port, and for the reception of the new settlement. The French ships had come to anchor in Botany Bay just before the departure of the *Sirius*; and during the intercourse which then took place, M. la Perouse had expressed a strong desire of having some letters conveyed to Europe. Governor Phillip was no sooner informed of this, than he dispatched an officer to him with full information of the time when it was probable our ships would sail, and with assurances that his letters should be punctually transmitted. By this officer the following intelligence was brought back concerning the voyage of the *Astrolabe* and *Boussole*.

These vessels had sailed from France in June 1785. They had touched at the Isle of Santa Catharina on the coast of Brasil, from thence had gone by the extremity of South America into the Pacific Ocean, where they had run along by the coasts of Chili and California. They had afterwards visited Easter Island, Nootka Sound, Cook's River, Kamschatka, Manilla, the Isles des Navigateurs, Sandwich and the Friendly Islands. M. la Perouse had also anchored off Norfolk Island, but could not land, on account of the surf. In this long voyage he had not lost any of his people by sickness; but two boats crews had unfortunately perished in a surf on the north-west coast of America; and at Masuna, one of the Isles des Navigateurs, M. L'Angle, Captain of the *Astrolabe*, had met with a fate still more unfortunate. That officer had gone ashore with two long boats for the purpose of filling some water casks. His party amounted to forty men, and the natives, from whom the French had received abundance of refreshments, and with whom they had been uniformly on the best terms, did not on their landing show any signs of a change of disposition. Malice unprovoked, and treachery without a motive, seem inconsistent even with the manners of savages; the French officers therefore, confiding in this unbroken state of amity, had suffered their boats to lie aground. But whether it were that the friendly behaviour of the natives had proceeded only from fear, or that some unknown offence had been given, they seized the moment when the men were busied in getting out the boats, to make an attack equally furious and unexpected. The assault was made with stones, of which prodigious numbers were thrown with extraordinary force and accuracy of direction. To this treachery M. L'Angle fell a sacrifice, and with him twelve of his party, officers and men, the long-boats were destroyed, and the remainder of those who had gone ashore escaped with difficulty in their small boats. The ships in the mean time were under sail, and having passed a point of land that intercepted the view, knew nothing of this melancholy and unaccountable affray till the boats returned. This fatal result from too implicit a confidence, may, perhaps very properly, increase the caution of Europeans in their commerce with savages, but ought not to excite suspicion. The resentments of such people are sudden and sanguinary, and, where the intercourse of language is wanting, may easily be awakened by misapprehension: but it seems possible to treat them with sufficient marks of confidence, without abandoning the guards of prudence. Offence is often given by the men, while the officers are most studious to preserve harmony, and against the transports of rage which arise on such occasions, it is always necessary to be prepared. Perhaps, also, a degree of awe should always be kept up, even to preserve their friendship. It has been uniformly remarked by our people, that defenceless stragglers are generally ill-treated by the natives of New South Wales, while towards parties armed and on their guard, they behave in the most amicable manner.

The debarkation was now made at Sydney Cove, and the work of clearing the ground for the encampment, as well as for the storehouses and other buildings, was begun without loss of time. But the labour which attended this necessary operation was greater than can easily be imagined by those who were not spectators of it. The coast, as well as the neighbouring country in general, is covered with wood; and though in this spot the trees stood more apart, and were less incumbered with underwood than in many other places, yet their magnitude was such as to render not only the felling, but the removal of them afterwards, a task of no small difficulty. By the habitual indolence of the convicts, and the want of proper overseers to keep them to their duty, their labour was rendered less efficient than it might have been.

26 January 1788

In the evening of the 26th the colours were displayed on shore, and the Governor, with several of his principal officers and others, assembled round the flag-staff, drank the king's health, and success to the settlement, with all that display of form which on such occasions is esteemed propitious, because it enlivens the spirits, and fills the imagination with pleasing presages. From this time to the end of the first week in February all was hurry and exertion. They who gave orders and they who received them were equally occupied; nor is it easy to conceive a busier scene than this part of the coast exhibited during the continuance of these first efforts towards establishment. The plan of the encampment was quickly formed, and places were marked out for every different purpose, so as to introduce, as much as possible, strict order and regularity. The materials and frame work to construct a slight temporary habitation for the Governor, had been brought out from England ready formed: these were landed and put together with as much expedition as the circumstances would allow. Hospital tents were also without delay erected, for which there was soon but too much occasion. In the passage from the Cape there had been but little sickness, nor had many died even among the convicts; but soon after landing, a dysentery prevailed, which in several instances proved fatal, and the scurvy began to rage with a virulence which kept the hospital tents generally supplied with patients. For those afflicted with this disorder, the advantage of fish or other fresh provisions could but rarely be procured; nor were esculent vegetables often obtained in sufficient plenty to produce any material alleviation of the complaint. In the dysentery, the red gum of the tree which principally abounds on this coast, was found a very powerful remedy. The yellow gum has been discovered to possess the same property, but in an inferior degree.

The tree which yields the former kind of gum is very considerable in size, and grows to a great height before it puts out any branches. The red gum is usually compared to that called sanguis draconis, but differs from it by being perfectly soluble in water, whereas the other, being more properly a resin, will not dissolve except in spirits of wine. It may be drawn from the tree by tapping, or taken out of the veins of the wood when dry, in which it is copiously distributed. The leaves are long and narrow, not unlike those of a willow. The wood is heavy and fine grained, but being much intersected by the channels containing the gum, splits and warps in such a manner as soon to become entirely useless; especially when worked up, as necessity at first occasioned it to be, without having been properly seasoned.

The yellow gum as it is called, is strictly a resin, not being at all soluble in water; in appearance it strongly resembles gamboge, but has not the property of staining. The plant that produces it is low and small, with long grassy leaves; but the fructification of it shoots out in a singular manner from the centre of the leaves, on a single straight stem, to the height of twelve or fourteen feet. Of this stem, which is strong and light, like some of the reed class, the natives usually make their spears; sometimes pointing them with a piece of the same substance made sharp, but more frequently with bone. The resin is generally dug up out of the soil under the tree, not collected from it, and may perhaps be that which Tasman calls "gum lac of the ground." The form of this plant is very exactly delineated in the annexed plate, and its proportion to other trees

17

may be collected from the plate, entitled, A View in New South Wales, in which many of this species are introduced.

Yellow Gum Plant
The month of February was ushered in by a very violent storm of thunder and rain. The lightning struck and shivered a tree, under which a shed had been erected for some sheep, and five of those animals were at the same time unfortunately destroyed by it. The encampment still went on with great alacrity, so that in the beginning of this month the work of building public storehouses was undertaken; and unremitting diligence began, though very gradually, to triumph over the obstacles which the nature of the place presented.

Chapter VIII.
February 1788

Description of Port Jackson and the adjacent country--The Governor's commission read--his Speech--his humane resolutions respecting the Natives--difficulties in erecting huts and other buildings--departure of Lieutenant King to Norfolk Island. A View in Port Jackson.

Port Jackson was not visited or explored by Captain Cook; it was seen only at the distance of between two or three miles from the coast: had any good fortune conducted him into that harbour, he would have found it much more worthy of his attention as a seaman, than that in which he passed a week. Governor Phillip himself pronounces it to be a harbour, in extent and security, superior to any he has ever seen: and the most experienced navigators who were with him fully concur in that opinion. From an entrance not more than two miles across, Port Jackson gradually extends into a noble and capacious bason; having soundings sufficient for the largest vessels, and space to accommodate, in perfect security, any number that could be assembled. It runs chiefly in a western direction, about thirteen miles into the country, and contains not less than an hundred small coves, formed by narrow necks of land, whose projections afford admirable shelter from all winds. Sydney Cove lies on the South side of the harbour, between five and six miles from the entrance. The necks of land that form the coves are mostly covered with timber, yet so rocky that it is not easy to comprehend how the trees could have found sufficient nourishment to bring them to so considerable a magnitude; but the soil between the rocks is very good, and into those spaces the principal roots have found their way. The soil in other parts of the coast immediately about Port Jackson is of various qualities. That neck of land which divides the south end of the harbour from the sea is chiefly sand. Between Sydney Cove and Botany Bay the first space is occupied by a wood, in some parts a mile and a half, in others three miles across; beyond that, is a kind of heath, poor, sandy, and full of swamps. As far as the eye can reach to the westward, the country is one continued wood. The head of the bay in Port Jackson, seemed at first to offer some advantages of ground, but as it is partly left dry at low water, and as the winds are much obstructed there by the woods and by the windings of the channel, it was deemed that it must probably be unhealthful, till the country can be cleared.

View in Port Jackson
There are several parts of the harbour in which the trees stand at a greater distance from each other than in Sydney Cove; some of these which have small runs of water, and a promising soil, Governor Phillip purposed to cultivate as soon as hands could be spared; but the advantage of being able to land the stores and provisions with so much ease, unavoidably determined his choice of a place for the principal settlement. Had it been attempted to remove those necessaries only one mile from the spot where they were landed, the undertaking probably would have been fruitless; so many were the obstacles to land carriage. At the head of Sydney Cove, therefore, Governor Phillip had fixed the seat of his government; but intent upon providing the best and earliest accommodation for those who were to be encamped with him; and wholly occupied by the continual necessity of giving directions, he had not yet found leisure for assuming regularly his powers and title of Governor. At length the hurry of the first preparations gave way to this more tranquil business.

7 February 1788

The 7th of February, 1788, was the memorable day which established a regular form of Government on the coast of New South Wales. For obvious reasons, all possible solemnity was given to the proceedings necessary on this occasion. On a space previously cleared, the whole colony was assembled; the military drawn up, and under arms; the convicts stationed apart; and near the person of the Governor, those who were to hold the principal offices under him. The Royal Commission was then read by Mr. D. Collins, the Judge Advocate. By this instrument Arthur Phillip was constituted and appointed Captain General and Governor in Chief in and over the territory, called New South Wales; extending from the northern cape, or extremity of the coast, called Cape York, in the latitude of ten degrees, thirty-seven minutes south, to the southern extremity of the said territory of New South Wales, or South Cape, in the latitude of forty-three degrees, thirty-nine minutes south, and of all the country inland to the westward, as far as the one hundred and thirty-fifth degree of east longitude, reckoning from the meridian of Greenwich, including all the islands adjacent in the Pacific Ocean, within the latitudes aforesaid of 10°. 37'. south, and 43°. 39'. south, and of all towns, garrisons, castles, forts, and all other fortifications, or other military works which may be hereafter erected upon the said territory, or any of the said islands. The act of Parliament establishing the courts of judicature was next read; and lastly, the patents under the great seal, empowering the proper persons to convene and hold those courts whenever the exigency should require. The Office of Lieutenant Governor was conferred on Major Ross, of the Marines. A triple discharge of musquetry concluded this part of the ceremony; after which Governor Phillip advanced, and addressing first the private soldiers, thanked them for their steady good conduct on every occasion: an honour which was repeated to them in the next general orders. He then turned to the convicts, and distinctly explained to them the nature of their present situation. The greater part, he bade them recollect, had already forfeited their lives to the justice of their country: yet, by the lenity of its laws, they were now so placed that, by industry and good behaviour, they might in time regain the advantages and estimation in society of which they had deprived themselves. They not only had every encouragement to make that effort, but were removed almost entirely from every temptation to guilt. There was little in this infant community which one man could plunder from another, and any dishonest attempts in so small a society would almost infallibly be discovered. To persons detected in such crimes, he could not promise any mercy; nor indeed to any whom, under their circumstances, should presume to offend against the peace and good order of the settlement. What mercy could do for them they had already experienced; nor could any good be now expected from those whom neither past warnings, nor the peculiarities of their present situation could preserve from guilt. Against offenders, therefore, the rigour of the law would certainly be put in force: while they whose behaviour should in any degree promise reformation, might always depend upon encouragement fully proportioned to their deserts. He particularly noticed the illegal intercourse between the sexes as an offence which encouraged a general profligacy of manners, and was in several ways injurious to society. To prevent this, he strongly recommended marriage, and promised every kind of countenance and assistance to those who, by entering into that state, should manifest their willingness to conform to the laws of morality and religion. Governor Phillip concluded his address, by declaring his earnest desire to promote the happiness of all who were under his government, and to render the settlement in New South Wales advantageous and honourabe to his country.

This speech, which was received with universal acclamations, terminated the ceremonial peculiar to the day. Nor was it altogether without its proper effect: For we are informed, that in the course of the ensuing week fourteen marriages took place among the convicts. The assembly was now dispersed, and the Governor proceeded to review the troops on the ground cleared for a parade: after which, he gave a dinner to the officers, and the first evening of his government was concluded propitiously, in good order and innocent festivity, amidst the repetition of wishes for its prosperity.

A rising government could not easily be committed to better hands. Governor Phillip appears to have every requisite to ensure the success of the undertaking intrusted to him, as far as the qualities of one man can ensure it. Intelligent, active, persevering with firmness to make his authority respected, and mildness to render it pleasing, he was determined, if possible, to bring even the native inhabitants of New South Wales into a voluntary subjection; or at least to establish with them a strict amity and alliance. Induced also by motives of humanity, it was his determination from his first landing, to treat them with the utmost kindness: and he was firmly resolved, that, whatever differences might arise, nothing less than the most absolute necessity should ever compel him to fire upon them. In this resolution, by good fortune, and by his own great address, he has happily been enabled to persevere. But notwithstanding this, his intentions of establishing a friendly intercourse have hitherto been frustrated. M. De la Peyrouse,* while he remained in Botany Bay, had some quarrel with the inhabitants, which unfortunately obliged him to use his fire-arms against them: this affair, joined to the ill behaviour of some of the convicts, who in spite of all prohibitions, and at the risque of all consequences, have wandered out among them, has produced a shyness on their parts which it has not yet been possible to remove, though the properest means have been taken to regain their confidence. Their dislike to the Europeans is probably increased by discovering that they intend to remain among them, and that they interfere with them in some of their best fishing places, which doubtless are, in their circumstances, objects of very great importance. Some of the convicts who have straggled into the woods have been killed, and others dangerously wounded by the natives, but there is great reason to suppose that in these cases the convicts have usually been the aggressors.

[* This is the right form of that officer's name; it was printed otherwise in a former passage by mistake.]

As the month of February advanced heavy rains began to fall, which pointed out the necessity of procuring shelter for the people as soon as possible. To have expedited this work in the degree which was desirable a great number of artificers would have been required. But this advantage could not be had. Only sixteen carpenters could be hired from all the ships; among the convicts no more than twelve were of this profession, and of them several were sick. These therefore together formed but a small party, in proportion to the work which was to be done. One hundred convicts were added as labourers; but with every effort, it was found impossible to complete either the barracks for the men, or the huts for the officers, as soon as was desired. As late as the middle of May these were yet unfinished, as well as the hospital, and the storehouse for those provisions which were not landed at first. The Governor himself at that time was still lodged in his temporary house of canvas, which was not perfectly impervious either to wind or weather.

14 February 1788.

On the 14th of February a party was sent out in the *Supply*, to settle on a small island to the north-west of New Zealand, in latitude 29° south, and longitude 168°. 10'. east from London, which was discovered and much commended by Captain Cook, and by him named Norfolk Island, in honour of the noble family to which that title belongs. To the office of superintendant and commandant of this island, and the settlement to be made upon it, Governor Phillip appointed Philip Gidley King, second lieutenant of his Majesty's ship *Sirius*, an officer much esteemed by him as of great merit in his profession; and highly spoken of in his letters as a man, whose perseverance in that or any other service might fully be depended on. As it was known that there were no inhabitants on Norfolk Island, there was sent with Lieut. King only a small detachment, consisting of one subaltern officer, and six marines, a very promising young man who was a midshipman, a surgeon,* two men who understood the cultivation and dressing of flax, with nine men and six women convicts. That the nature of this settlement may be fully understood, a copy of the instructions delivered to Mr. King at his departure is subjoined to this chapter.

[* The surgeon's name is Jamison, whose intelligent letters to Lewis Wolfe, Esq; were kindly lent to the publisher, and have afforded much useful information.]

INSTRUCTIONS for PHILIP GIDLEY KING, Esq; Superintendant and Commandant of the Settlement of NORFOLK ISLAND.

With these instructions you will receive my Commission, appointing you to superintend and command the settlement to be formed in Norfolk Island, and to obey all such orders as you shall from time to time receive from me, his Majesty's Governor in Chief, and Captain General of the territory of New South Wales and its dependencies, or from the Lieutenant-Governor in my absence.

You are therefore to proceed in his Majesty's armed tender *Supply*, whose commander has my orders to receive you, with the men and women, stores and provisions necessary for forming the intended settlement; and on your landing on Norfolk Island you are to take upon you the execution of the trust reposed in you, causing my commission, appointing you superintendant over the said settlement, to be publicly read.

After having taken the necessary measures for securing yourself and people, and for the preservation of the stores and provisions, you are immediately to proceed to the cultivation of the Flax Plant, which you will find growing spontaneously on the island: as likewise to the cultivation of cotton, corn, and other plants, with the seeds of which you are furnished, and which you are to regard as public stock, and of the increase of which you are to send me an account, that I may know what quantity may be drawn from the island for public use, or what supplies it may be necessary to send hereafter. It is left to your discretion to use such part of the corn that is raised as may be found necessary; but this you are to do with the greatest oeconomy; and as the corn, flax, cotton, and other grains are the property of the Crown, and as such are to be accounted for, you are to keep an exact account of the increase, and you will in future receive directions for the disposal thereof.

You are to inform yourself of the nature of the soil, what proportion of land you find proper for the cultivation of corn, flax, and cotton, as likewise what quantity of cattle may be bred on the island, and the number of people you judge necessary for the above purpose. You will likewise observe what are the prevailing winds in the different seasons of the year, the best anchorage according to the season, the rise and fall of the tides, likewise when the dry and rainy seasons begin and end.

You will be furnished with a four oared boat, and you are not on any consideration to build, or to permit the building of any vessel or boat whatever that is decked; or of any boat or vessel that is not decked, whose length of keel exceeds twenty feet: and if by any accident any vessel or boat that exceeds twenty feet keel should be driven on the island, you are immediately to cause such boat or vessel to be scuttled, or otherwise rendered unserviceable, letting her remain in that situation until you receive further directions from me.

You will be furnished with six months provisions, within which time you will receive an additional supply, but as you will be able to procure fish and vegetables, you are to endeavour to make the provisions you receive serve as long as possible.

The convicts being the servants of the Crown, till the time for which they are sentenced is expired, their labour is to be for the public; and you are to take particular notice of their general good or bad behaviour, that they may hereafter be employed or rewarded according to their different merits.

You are to cause the Prayers of the Church of England to be read with all due solemnity every Sunday, and you are to inforce a due observance of religion and good order, transmitting to me, as often as opportunity offers, a full account of your particular situation and transactions.

You are not to permit any intercourse or trade with any ships or vessels that may stop at the island, whether English or of any other nation, unless such ships or vessels should be in distress, in which case you are to afford them such assistance as may be in your power.

Given under my hand, at Head Quarters in Port Jackson, New South Wales, this 12th day of February, 1788.

(Signed)

ARTHUR PHILLIP.

Chapter IX.

February 1788 to March 1788

A Criminal Court held--Broken Bay explored by Governor Phillip--Interviews with the Natives--Peculiarities remarked--Friendly behaviour and extraordinary courage of an old man.

Governor Phillip soon found with great regret, though doubtless without much surprise, that in the community committed to his care the strict enforcement of the sanctions of law was peculiarly necessary. There were in it many individuals whom neither lenity could touch, nor rigour terrify; who, with all sense of social duty, appeared to have lost all value for life itself, and with the same wantonness exposed themselves to the darts of the savages, and to the severe punishments which, however reluctantly, every society must inflict when milder methods have been tried without success. Towards the latter end of February a criminal court was convened, in which six of the convicts received sentence of death. One, who was the head of the gang, was executed the same day; of the rest, one was pardoned; the other four were reprieved, and afterwards exiled to a small island within the bay, where they were kept on bread and water. These men had frequently robbed the stores, and the other convicts. He who suffered, and two others, had been detected in stealing from the stores the very day that they had received a week's provision; at a time when their allowance, as settled by the Navy Board, was the same as that of the soldiers, spirituous liquors excepted. So inveterate were their habits of dishonesty, that even the apparent want of a motive could not repress them.

2 March 1788

On the 2d of March Governor Phillip went with a long boat and cutter to examine the broken land, mentioned by Captain Cook, about eight miles to the northward of Port Jackson, and by him named Broken Bay. This bay proved to be very extensive. The first night they slept in the boats, within a rocky point in the north-west part of the bay, as the natives, though friendly, appeared to be numerous; and the next day, after passing a bar that had only water for small vessels, they entered a very extensive branch, from which the ebb tide came out so strong that the boats could not row against it in the stream; and here was deep water. This opening appeared to end in several small branches, and in a large lagoon which could not then be examined, as there was not time to seek a channel for the boats among the banks of sand and mud. Most of the land in the upper part of this branch was low and full of swamps. Pelicans and various other birds were here seen in great numbers. Among the rest an uncommon kind, called then the Hooded Gull, and supposed to be a non descript; but it appears from a drawing sent to England, a plate from which is here inserted, to be of that species called by Mr. Latham the Caspian Tern, and is described by him as the second variety of that species.*

[* Latham's Synopsis of Birds, vol. vi. p. 351.]

Caspian Tern

Leaving this north-west branch they proceeded across the bay, and went into the south-west branch. This is also very extensive; and from it runs a second opening to the westward, affording shelter for almost any number of ships. In this part, as far as could then be examined, there is water for vessels of the greatest burthen, the soundings being at the entrance seven fathoms, and in going up still more. Continual rains prevented them from taking a survey. The land here was found much higher than at Port Jackson, more rocky, and equally covered with timber. Large trees were seen growing even on the summits of the mountains, which appeared accessible only to birds. Immediately round the headland that forms the southern entrance into the bay, there is a third branch, which Governor Phillip thought the finest piece of water he had ever seen; and which therefore he thought worthy to be honoured with the name of Pitt Water. This, as well as the south-west branch, is of sufficient extent to contain all the navy of Great Britain. But on a narrow bar which runs across the entrance it has only eighteen feet depth at low water. Within the bar there are from seven to fifteen fathoms. The land is not so high in this part as in the south-west branch, and there are some good situations where the land might be cultivated. Small springs of water were seen in most of the coves, and three cascades falling from heights, which the rains at that time rendered inaccessible.

In this excursion some interviews with the natives took place. When the party first landed in Broken Bay several women came down to the beach with the men. One of these, a young woman, was very talkative and remarkably cheerful. This was a singular instance, for in general they are observed on this coast to be much less cheerful than the men, and apparently under great awe and subjection. They certainly are not treated with much tenderness, and it is thought that they are employed chiefly in the canoes, in which women have frequently been seen with very young children at the breast. The lively young lady, when she joined the party the second day in her canoe, stood up and gave a song which was far from unpleasing. The men very readily gave their assistance to the English in making a fire, and behaved in the most friendly manner. In a bay where Governor Phillip and his company landed to draw the seine, a number of the natives again came to them. It was now first observed by the Governor that the women in general had lost two joints from the little finger of the left hand. As these appeared to be all married women, he at first conjectured this privation to be a part of the marriage ceremony; but going afterwards into a hut where were several women and children, he saw a girl of five or six years of age whose left hand was thus mutilated; and at the same time an old woman, and another who appeared to have had children, on both of whom all the fingers were perfect. Several instances were afterwards observed of women with child, and of others that were evidently wives, who had not lost the two joints, and of children from whom they had been cut. Whatever be the occasion of this mutilation, it is performed on females only; and considering the imperfection of their instruments, must be a very painful operation. Nothing has been seen in the possession of these people that is at all calculated for performing such an amputation, except a shell fixed to a short stick, and used generally for pointing their spears, or for separating the oysters from the rocks. More fingers than one are never cut; and in every instance it is the same finger that has suffered.*

[* In Patterson's Travels in Africa, lately published, we are told, that he met with a tribe of Hottentots near Orange River, all of whom had lost the first joint of the little finger: the reason they gave for cutting it off was, that it was a cure for a particular sickness to which they were subject when young. Fourth Journey, p. 117. It would be a curious coincidence of customs should it be discovered that the natives of New Holland do it for any similar reason.]

The men are distinguished in a different manner: their fingers are not mutilated, but most of them, as other voyagers have observed, want the right front tooth in the upper jaw. Governor Phillip having remarked this, pointed out to them that he had himself lost one of his front teeth, which occasioned a general clamour; and it was thought he derived some merit in their opinion from this circumstance. The perforation of the cartilage that divides the nostrils, and the strange disfiguring ornament of a long bone or stick thrust through it, was now observed, as described by Captain Cook; and the same appellation of sprit-sail yard, was ludicrously applied to it by the sailors. But several very old men were seen in this excursion who had not lost the tooth, nor had their noses prepared to receive that grotesque appendage: probably, therefore, these are marks of distinction: ambition must have its badges, and where cloaths are not worn, the body itself must be compelled to bear them.

Whether the scars raised upon the skin were of this kind, or as Captain Cook understood by their signs, marks of sorrow for deceased friends, could not now be learnt. They are of a very singular nature: sometimes the skin is raised from the flesh for several inches, appearing as if it were filled with wind, and forming a round surface of more than a quarter of an inch diameter. Their bodies are scarred in various parts, particularly about the breast and arms, and frequently on the instep. Nor does the head always escape; one man in particular, putting aside the hair on the forepart of his head, showed a scar, and then pointing to one on the foot, and to others on different parts of the body, seemed to intimate that he thought himself much honoured by having these marks upon him from head to foot. The women did not appear equally forward to produce the mutilated finger; nor was it always possible to ascertain whether they had lost the joints or not. For though they made no attempt to secrete themselves, nor seemed impressed with any idea that one part of the body more requires concealment than another, yet there was a shyness and timidity among them which frequently kept them at a distance. They never would approach so readily as the men, and sometimes would not even land from their canoes, but made signs that what was offered should be given to the men. We are not yet enough acquainted with the manners of the people to decide whether this reserve proceeds from the fears of the women, or from the jealousy of their husbands, by whom they are evidently kept in great subordination.

One of their modes of fishing was now observed: their hooks are made of the inside of a shell resembling mother of pearl. When a fish which has taken the bait is supposed to be too strong to be landed with the line, the canoe is paddled to shore, and while one man gently draws the fish along, another stands prepared to strike it with a spear: in this attempt they seldom fail. In the plate which represents this action, the engraver has inadvertently left the bodies of the figures rather too white; in other respects it is very accurate.

Natives of Botany Bay

When the southern branch of Broken Bay was first visited, the getting round the headland that separates the branches, was attended with some difficulty, on account of very heavy squalls of wind, accompanied with rain. An attempt was made to land, where there proved not to be sufficient water for the boat. During this transaction, an old man and a youth were standing on the rocks where the boat was trying to approach. Having seen how much our men had laboured to get under land, they were very solicitous to point out the deepest water. Afterwards they brought fire, and seemed willing to render any service in their power. Two of the officers suffered themselves to be conducted by the old man to a cave at some distance, but declined going in, though he invited them by all the signs he could invent. This was rather unfortunate, as the rain was falling very violently, and the cave was found next day sufficiently large to have sheltered the whole party. The old man certainly took great pains to make this understood, but the motive of his earnestness unluckily was mistaken, and his visitors suffered for their suspicions. He afterwards assisted in clearing away the bushes, and making preparations for the party to sleep on shore, and next morning was rewarded with presents for his very friendly behaviour. Two days afterwards, when Governor Phillip returned to the same spot, the old man met him with a dance and a song of joy. His son was with him, and several of the natives; a hatchet was given them and other presents; and as the Governor was to return next day to Port Jackson, it was hoped that the friendship thus begun, and so studiously cultivated, would have continued firm. But as soon as it was dark, the old man stole a spade, and was caught with it in his hand. Governor Phillip thought it necessary, on this occasion, to shew some tokens of displeasure, and therefore when the delinquent approached, he gave him two or three slight slaps on the shoulder, and then pushed him away, at the same time pointing to the spade. This gentle chastisement at once destroyed their friendship. The old man immediately seized a spear, and coming close up to the Governor, poized it, and seemed determined to strike. But seeing that his threats were disregarded, (for his antagonist chose rather to risk the effects of his anger than to fire upon him) or perhaps dissuaded by something the other natives said, in a few moments he dropped the spear and went away. It was impossible not to be struck with the courage displayed by him on this occasion, for Governor Phillip at the time was not alone, but had several officers and men about him. From this and other similar events, personal bravery appears to be a quality in which the natives of New South Wales are not by any means deficient. The old man returned the next morning with many other natives, but, in order to convince him of his fault, he was less noticed than his companions, who were presented with hatchets and various other articles.

9 March 1788

It was now the 9th of March, and Governor Phillip returned to Port Jackson: having gained some useful knowledge of the country, and maintained an intercourse with the natives without departing from his favourite plan of treating them with the utmost kindness. He had endeavoured at the same time to gain their confidence, if possible, and secure their friendship. If these humane endeavours were afterwards rendered fruitless by the wanton profligacy of some depraved individuals, however he might regret it, he could have no reason to reproach himself.

The rain, which was almost constant, prevented the Governor from returning by land, which otherwise he meant to have done, for the sake of exploring a part of the country which appeared to be good and free from timber.

Chapter X.

March 1788

Departure of the French Ships--Death of M. Le Receveur--Return of the *Supply* from Norfolk Island--Description of that Place--Howe Island discovered.

10 March 1788

On the 10th of March, the French ships sailed from Botany Bay. M. De la Peyrouse during his stay there had set up two long boats, the frames of which he had brought with him from Europe. There had not been much intercourse between the French and English in this interval: both being too busily employed to waste their time in parties of pleasure. Captain Clonard had waited on Governor Phillip with the letters which were to be forwarded to the French ambassador; and a few of the English officers had gone over by land about the same time to pay a visit in Botany Bay; both parties were of course received with politeness and hospitality. Some few of the convicts contrived to abscond, and endeavoured to get admitted into the French ships, but were, with great propriety, rejected. Those vessels returned towards the north, where they were to make another voyage.

Chart of Norfolk Island

During the stay of M. De la Peyrouse in Botany Bay, Father Le Receveur, who had come out in the *Astrolabe* as a naturalist, died. His death was occasioned by wounds which he received in the unfortunate rencounter at the Navigator's Islands. A slight monument was erected to his memory, with the following inscription.

Hic jacet LE RECEVEUR, E. F. F. Minimis Galliae Sacerdos, Physicus in circumnavigatione Mundi, Duce DE LA PEYROUSE, Ob. 17 Feb. 1788.

The monument being soon after destroyed by the natives, Governor Phillip caused the inscription to be engraved on copper, and affixed to a neighbouring tree. M. De la Peyrouse had paid a similar tribute of respect to the memory of Captain Clerke, at the harbour of St. Peter and Paul in Kamtschatka.

19 March 1788

On the 19th of this month, Lieutenant Ball arrived in the *Supply* from Norfolk Island. He had made that island on the 29th of February, but was five days off the coast before a place could be found at which it was possible to land the stores and provisions. So completely do the rocks surround the island, that it was not easy to find a place even to land a man. At length, however, they succeeded, having discovered at the south-west end, a small opening in a reef that runs across a bay. Here the people, provisions and stores were all put on shore in perfect safety. The Commandant wrote in high spirits at the promising appearance of his new territory; and subsequent accounts have proved, that the opinion he then formed was not erroneous. He described Norfolk Island as one entire wood, or rather as a garden overrun with the noblest pines, in straightness, size, and magnitude, far superior to any he had ever seen. Nothing can exceed the fertility of its soil. Wherever it has been since examined, a rich black mould has been found to the depth of five or six feet: and the grain and garden seeds which have been sown, such only excepted as were damaged in the carriage, or by the weevil, have vegetated with the utmost luxuriance. To prevent repetitions, it may perhaps be best to unite in this place the accounts which have been received of this island, though many of them will easily be perceived to be greatly posterior to this first return of the *Supply*.

Norfolk Island is about seven leagues in circumference, and if not originally formed, like many other small islands, by the eruption of volcanic matter from the bed of the sea, must doubtless have contained a volcano. This conclusion is formed from the vast quantity of pumice stone which is scattered in all parts of it, and mixed with the soil. The crater, or at least some traces of its former existence, will probably be found at the summit of a small mountain, which rises near the middle of the island. To this mountain the Commandant has given the name of Mount Pitt. The island is exceedingly well watered. At, or near Mount Pitt, rises a strong and copious stream, which flowing through a very fine valley, divides itself into several branches, each of which retains sufficient force to be used in turning mills: and in various parts of the island excellent springs have been discovered.

The climate is pure, salubrious, and delightful, preserved from oppressive heats by constant breezes from the sea, and of so mild a temperature throughout the winter, that vegetation continues there without interruption, one crop succeeding another. Refreshing showers from time to time maintain perpetual verdure; not indeed of grass, for none has yet been seen upon the island, but of the trees, shrubs, and other vegetables which in all parts grow abundantly. On the leaves of these, and of some kinds in particular, the sheep, hogs, and goats, not only live, but thrive and fatten very much. To the salubrity of the air every individual in this little colony can bear ample testimony, from the uninterrupted state of good health which has been in general enjoyed.

When our settlers landed, there was not a single acre clear of wood in the island, and the trees were so bound together by that kind of creeping shrub called supple jack, interwoven in all directions, as to render it very difficult to penetrate far among them. The Commandant, small as his numbers were at first, by indefatigable activity soon caused a space to be cleared sufficient for the requisite accommodations, and for the production of esculent vegetables of all kinds in the greatest abundance. When the last accounts arrived, three acres of barley were in a very thriving state, and ground was prepared to receive rice and Indian corn. In the wheat there had been a disappointment, the grain that was sown having been so much injured by the weevil, as to be unfit for vegetation. But the people were all at that time in commodious houses; and, according to the declarations of Mr. King himself, in his letters to Governor Phillip, there was not a doubt that this colony would be in a situation to support itself entirely without assistance, in less than four years: and with very little in the intermediate time. Even two years would be more than sufficient for this purpose, could a proper supply of black cattle be sent.

Fish are caught in great plenty, and in the proper season very fine turtle. The woods are inhabited by innumerable tribes of birds, many of them very gay in plumage. The most useful are pigeons, which are very numerous, and a bird not unlike the Guinea fowl, except in colour, (being chiefly white,) both of which were at first so tame as to suffer themselves to be taken by hand. Of plants that afford vegetables for the table, the chief are cabbage palm, the wild plantain, the fern tree, a kind of wild spinage, and a tree which produces a diminutive fruit, bearing some resemblance to a currant. This, it is hoped, by transplanting and care, will be much improved in size and flavour.

But the productions which give the greatest importance to Norfolk Island are the pines and the flax plant, the former rising to a size and perfection unknown in other places, and promising the most valuable supply of masts and spars for our navy in the East Indies; the latter not less estimable for the purposes of making sail-cloth, cordage, and even the finest manufactures; growing in great plenty, and with such luxuriance as to attain the height of eight feet.* The pines measure frequently one hundred and sixty, or even one hundred and eighty feet in height, and are sometimes nine or ten feet in diameter at the bottom of the trunk. They rise to about eighty feet without a branch; the wood is said to be of the best quality, almost as light as that of the best Norway masts; and the turpentine obtained from it is remarkable for purity and whiteness. The fern tree is found also of a great height for its species, measuring from seventy to eighty feet, and affords excellent food for the sheep and other small cattle. A plant producing pepper, and supposed to be the true oriental pepper, has been discovered lately in the island, growing in great plenty; and specimens have been sent to England, in order to ascertain this important point.

[* The flax plant is thus described in Captain Cook's first voyage, vol. iii. p. 39. as found at New Zealand. "There is, however, a plant that serves the inhabitants instead of hemp and flax, which excels all that are put to the same purposes in other countries. Of this plant there are two sorts; the leaves of both resemble those of flags, but the flowers are smaller and their clusters more numerous; in one kind they are yellow, and in the other a deep red. Of the leaves of these plants, with very little preparation, they make all their common apparel; and of these they also make their strings, lines, and cordage for every purpose, which are so much stronger than any thing we can make with hemp, that they will not bear a comparison. From the same plant, by another preparation, they draw long slender fibres which shine like silk, and are as white as snow: of these, which are also surprizingly strong, the finer clothes are made; and of the leaves, without any other preparation than splitting them into proper breadths and trying the strips together, they make their fishing nets; some of which, as I have before remarked, are of an enormous size." It is added, that it is found in every kind of soil. It is perennial, and has a bulbous root. Some of the roots have lately been sent to England.]

The chief disadvantage experienced by those who are sent to Norfolk Island, is the want of a good landing place. The bay which has been used for this purpose is inclosed by a reef of coral rock, through which there is a passage only for a boat; and during the tide of flood, when the wind is westerly, the landing is rather dangerous. In one of the debarkations a midshipman, who was ordered to lie within the reef, that he might attend the boats coming to shore, imprudently suffered his own boat to drive into the surf, and was lost, with four men. He had been once before overset in consequence of a similar inattention, and then had lost one man. On the coast of the island are several small bays, and there are still hopes that a better landing place may be discovered; but the necessity of employing all the men in sheltering themselves and the stores from the weather, or in clearing ground for various purposes, has hitherto prevented Mr. King from sending out any persons to complete the examination. Should this enquiry prove unsuccessful, it is proposed to attempt the blowing up of one or two small rocks, by which the reef is rendered dangerous. If this expedient also should fail, the evil must be borne with patience. In summer the landing will generally be sufficiently secure; and seamen, who have seen the bay of Riga, in the Baltic, declare, that it will at all times be safer for a ship to load with masts and spars at Norfolk Island, than in that place, where so many ships are freighted yearly.

Rats are the only quadrupeds which have been found in this island; and from these, as well as from the ants, it was feared the crops might suffer; but no great inconvenience has yet been experienced from them; and proper exertions seldom fail in a short time to reduce the number of such enemies, enough to make their depredations very inconsiderable. On the whole, Norfolk Island certainly deserves to be considered as an acquisition of some importance, and is likely to answer even the most sanguine expectations. Some canoes have been found on the rocks, which were supposed to have been driven from New Zealand; but the appearance of a fresh cocoa nut and a small piece of manufactured wood, which seemed to have been only a small time in the water, has lately suggested an idea that probably some inhabited island may lie at no great distance. There has not been as yet any opportunity to determine whether this opinion be well founded or not.

A small island, but entirely uninhabited, was discovered by Lieutenant Ball in his passage to Norfolk Island. In his return he examined it, and found that the shore abounded with turtle, but there was no good anchorage. He named it Lord Howe Island. It is in 31° 36' south latitude, and 159° east longitude. Part of this island being very high may be seen at the distance of sixteen leagues, and a rock to the south-east of it, may be discerned even at eighteen leagues. In latitude 29° 25' south, longitude 159° 59' east, a very dangerous reef has since been seen. The ship from which it was observed was then four leagues to the southward, and it could not at that time be ascertained how far it extends to the northward.

To expedite the cultivation of Norfolk Island a fresh detachment was sent thither in October, consisting of an officer and eight marines, with thirty convicts, consisting of ten women and twenty men: Thus, there existed on this islet, when the last accounts were transmitted, forty-four men and sixteen women, who, having eighteen months provisions, lived comfortably on this sequestered spot, under the prudent management of a youthful ruler, of whose busy life the reader may wish to know all the particulars, which at present can be authentically told.

Philip Gidley King, who had the honour to conduct the original settlers to Norfolk Island, was born at Launceston in Cornwall, on the 23d of April, 1758. He is the son of Philip King, of that town, draper, who married the daughter of John Gidley, of Exeter, attorney at law. Much as he owes to his parents, he is indebted for his scholastic learning to Mr. Bailey at Yarmouth. He derives, probably, some advantages from making an early choice of his profession. At the age of twelve, he went to the East Indies on board the Swallow frigate, Captain Shirley, by whom he was rated a midshipman. From this station he returned to England, at the end of five years, with much knowledge of his business, and some acquaintance with the world. In 1775, he entered upon real service; and has continued in active employment from that period to this great epoch of his life. He went to Virginia with Captain Bellew, in the Liverpool, during the year 1775; with whom he continued till the shipwreck of that frigate in Delaware Bay. And having entered on board the Princess Royal, in October 1778, he was made a Lieutenant by Admiral Byron, in the Renown, on the 26th of November following. He returned to England in the subsequent year; and served in the Channel on board the Kite cutter, and Ariadne frigate, till the beginning of 1783. With Captain Phillip he went to the East Indies, as Lieutenant of the Europe, in January 1783; from whence he returned on the restoration of complete peace, in May 1784. In this service it was, that Phillip and King became acquainted with the merit of each other. And when the expedition to New South Wales was projected, King was appointed Lieutenant of the *Sirius*, on the 25th of October, 1786, at the same time that Phillip was nominated Commander of the voyage.

Lieutenant King
Chapter XI.
March 1788 to May 1788

Three of the transports cleared--Two excursions made into the country, on the fifteenth of April, and on the twenty-second--Huts of the natives--Sculpture, and other particulars.

25 March 1788

On the 25th of March, the *Charlotte*, *Lady Penrhyn*, and *Scarborough* transports, having been cleared of all their stores, were discharged from government service, and left at liberty to proceed for China, whenever their commanders should think proper. The other ships were of necessity detained till the store-houses could be finished.

15 April 1788

The month of April was not distinguished by any events that deserve to be related, except two expeditions of Governor Phillip for the purpose of exploring the country. On the first of these excursions he set out on the 15th with provisions for four days; attended by several officers, and a small party of marines. They landed at the head of a small cove, called Shell Cove, near the entrance of the harbour on the north side. Proceeding in this direction they arrived at a large lake, which they examined, though not without great labour. It was surrounded by a considerable extent of bog and marshy ground, in which, in the course of their progress, they were frequently plunged up to the waist. On this lake they first observed a black swan, which species, though proverbially rare in other parts of the world, is here by no means uncommon, being found on most of the lakes. This was a very noble bird, larger than the common swan, and equally beautiful in form. On being shot at, it rose and discovered that its wings were edged with white: the bill was tinged with red.

In three days, with great difficulty, they passed the swamps and marshes which lie near the harbour. Nothing can more fully point out the great improvement which may be made by the industry of a civilized people in this country, than the circumstances of the small streams which descend into Port Jackson. They all proceed from swamps produced by the stagnation of the water after rising from the springs. When the obstacles which impede their course can be removed, and free channels opened through which they may flow, the adjacent ground will gradually be drained, and the streams themselves will become more useful; at the same time habitable and salubrious situations will be gained in places where at present perpetual damps prevail, and the air itself appears to stagnate.

On leaving these low grounds, they found them succeeded by a rocky and barren country. The hills were covered with flowering shrubs, but by means of various obstacles the ascending and descending was difficult, and in many parts impracticable. At the distance of about fifteen miles from the sea coast Governor Phillip obtained a very fine view of the inland country and its mountains, to several of which he now gave names. The most northern of them he named Carmarthen Hills, the most southern Lansdown Hills; one which lay between these was called Richmond Hill. From the manner in which these mountains appeared to rise, it was thought almost certain that a large river must descend from among them. But it was now necessary to return, without making any further examination.

22 April 1788

On the 22d another excursion of the same kind was undertaken: Governor Phillip landed with his party near the head of the harbour. Here they found a good country, but in a short time arrived at a very close cover; and after passing the chief part of the day in fruitless attempts to make their way through it, were obliged to relinquish the attempt, and return. The next day, by keeping close to the banks of a small creek for about four miles, they contrived to pass the cover, and for the three succeeding days continued their course to the west-ward. The country through which they travelled was singularly fine, level, or rising in small hills of a very pleasing and picturesque appearance. The soil excellent, except in a few small spots where it was stony. The trees growing at the distance of from twenty to forty feet from each other, and in general entirely free from underwood, which was confined to the stony and barren spots. On the fifth day they ascended a small eminence, whence, for the first time in this second expedition, they saw Carmarthen and Lansdown Hills. The country round this hill was so beautiful, that Governor Phillip gave it the name of Belle-vue. They were still apparently thirty miles from the mountains which it had been their object to reach, and not having found it practicable, with the tents, arms, and other necessaries, to carry more than six days provisions, were obliged to return. Even with this small stock, the officers as well as men, had been under the necessity of carrying heavy loads. Water for the use of the day was always taken; for though it happened in every instance that pools of water were found which had remained after the rains, yet this was a supply on which they could not previously depend. The extraordinary difficulty of penetrating into this country had now been fully experienced; where unexpected delays from deep ravines and other obstacles, frequently force the traveller from his direct course, and baffle every conjecture concerning the time required for passing a certain tract. The utmost extent of this excursion in a direct line had not been more than thirty miles, and it had taken up five days. The return of the party was effected with much more ease; the track was made, and the trees marked the whole way where they had passed; with these assistances they reached their boats in a day and a half.

It was still the general opinion that the appearance of the country promised the discovery of a large river in that district, whenever the line now taken could be fully pursued. Another expedition was therefore planned, in which it was determined, if possible, to reach either Lansdown or Carmarthen Hills: and the hope of so important a discovery as that of a river made every one anxious to go, notwithstanding the great fatigue with which these undertakings were attended. But this design was for the present unavoidably deferred. Governor Phillip, who had not been perfectly well even at the time of setting out on the excursion to Broken Bay, had then contracted a severe pain in his side, by sleeping frequently on the wet ground. This complaint had in the two last journeys received so much increase, that he found it absolutely necessary to allow himself the respite of a few weeks, before he again encountered so much fatigue.

The country explored in this last journey was so good and so fit for the purposes of cultivation, that the Governor resolved to send a detachment to settle there, as soon as a sufficient number could be spared from works of more immediate necessity. But notwithstanding the goodness of the soil it is a matter of astonishment how the natives, who know not how to avail themselves of its fertility, can subsist in the inland country. On the coast fish makes a considerable part of their food, but where that cannot be had, it seems hardly possible that with their spears, the only missile weapon yet observed among them, they should be able to procure any kind of animal food. With the assistance of their guns the English gentlemen could not obtain, in the last six days they were out, more than was barely sufficient for two meals. Yet, that these parts are frequented by the natives was undeniably proved by the temporary huts which were seen in several places. Near one of these huts the bones of a kanguroo were found, and several trees were seen on fire. A piece of a root resembling that of the fern tree was also picked up by Governor Phillip; part of this root had been chewed, and so recently that it was thought it could not have been left many minutes. It seemed evident by several marks, that the natives had only fled at the approach of the English party, but so effectually did they conceal themselves that not one was seen.

Hut in New South Wales
The number of the natives in these inland parts must, however, be very small. Whether these reside by choice where they must encounter so many difficulties, or whether they are driven from the society of those who inhabit the coast, has not yet been discovered. The huts seen here consisted of single pieces of bark, about eleven feet in length, and from four to six in breadth, bent in the middle while fresh from the tree, and set up so as to form an acute angle, not a little resembling cards set up by children. In the plate inserted here, not only the huts, but some of the spears of the natives are introduced. It was conjectured, that the chief use of these imperfect structures might be, to conceal them from the animals for which they must frequently be obliged to lie in wait. They may also afford shelter from a shower of rain to one or two who sit or lie under them. The bark of many trees was observed to be cut into notches, as if for the purpose of climbing; and in several there were holes, apparently the retreat of some animal, but enlarged by the natives for the purpose of catching the inhabitant. The enlargement of these holes with their imperfect instruments, must itself be a work of time, and must require no little patience. In some places, where the hole was rather too high to be reached from the ground, boughs of trees were laid to facilitate the ascent. The animals that take refuge in those places are probably the squirrel, the opossum, or the kanguroo-rat. At the bottom of one of these trees, the skin of a flying squirrel was found.

In many places fires had lately been made; but in one only were seen any shells of oysters or muscles, and there not more than half a dozen. Fish-bones were not found at all, which seems to prove, that in their journies inland these people do not carry with them any provisions of that kind. Kanguroos were frequently seen, but were so shy that it was very difficult to shoot them. With respect to these animals, it is rather an extraordinary circumstance, that, notwithstanding their great shyness, and notwithstanding they are daily shot at, more of them are seen near the camp than in any other part of the country. The kanguroo, though it resembles the jerboa in the peculiarity of using only the hinder legs in progression, does not belong to that genus. The pouch of the female, in which the young are nursed, is thought to connect it rather with the opossum tribe. This extraordinary formation, hitherto esteemed peculiar to that one genus, seems, however, in New Holland not to be sufficiently characteristic: it has been found both in the rat and the squirrel kind. The largest kanguroo which has yet been shot weighed about one hundred and forty pounds. But it has been discovered that there are two kinds, one of which seldom exceeds sixty pounds in weight: these live chiefly on the high grounds: their hair is of a reddish cast, and the head is shorter than in the larger sort. Young kanguroos which have been taken, have in a few days grown very tame, but none have lived more than two or three weeks. Yet it is still possible that when their proper food shall be better known, they may be domesticated. Near some water, in this journey, was found the dung of an animal that fed on grass, which, it was supposed, could not have been less than a horse. A kanguroo, so much above the usual size, would have been an extraordinary phaenomenon, though no larger animal has yet been seen, and the limits of growth in that species are not ascertained. The tail of the kanguroo, which is very large, is found to be used as a weapon of offence, and has given such severe blows to dogs as to oblige them to desist from pursuit. Its flesh is coarse and lean, nor would it probably be used for food, where there was not a scarcity of fresh provisions. The disproportion between the upper and lower parts of this animal is greater than has been shown in any former delineations of it, but is well expressed in the plate inserted here.

The dimensions of a stuffed kanguroo in the possession of Mr. Nepean, are these,

28

f. in. Length from the point of the nose to the end of
the tail, 6   1 -- of the tail,   2   1 ----   head,
0   8 ----   fore legs,   1   0 ----   hinder legs,   2   8
Circumference of the forepart, by the legs,   1   1 ----   lower parts,   ----
3   2

The middle toe of the hind feet is remarkably long, strong, and sharp.

The Kanguroo

The natives of New South Wales, though in so rude and uncivilized a state as not even to have made an attempt towards clothing themselves, notwithstanding that at times they evidently suffer from the cold and wet, are not without notions of sculpture. In all these excursions of Governor Phillip, and in the neighbourhood of Botany Bay and Port Jackson, the figures of animals, of shields, and weapons, and even of men, have been seen carved upon the rocks, roughly indeed, but sufficiently well to ascertain very fully what was the the object intended. Fish were often represented, and in one place the form of a large lizard was sketched out with tolerable accuracy. On the top of one of the hills, the figure of a man in the attitude usually assumed by them when they begin to dance, was executed in a still superior style. That the arts of imitation and amusement, should thus in any degree precede those of necessity, seems an exception to the rules laid down by theory for the progress of invention. But perhaps it may better be considered as a proof that the climate is never so severe as to make the provision of covering or shelter a matter of absolute necessity. Had these men been exposed to a colder atmosphere, they would doubtless have had clothes and houses, before they attempted to become sculptors.

In all the country hitherto explored, the parties have seldom gone a quarter of a mile without seeing trees which had been on fire. As violent thunder storms are not uncommon on this coast, it is possible that they may have been burnt by lightning, which the gum-tree is thought particularly to attract; but it is probable also that they may have been set on fire by the natives. The gum-tree is highly combustible, and it is a common practice with them to kindle their fires at the root of one of these trees. When they quit a place they never extinguish the fire they have made, but leave it to burn out, or to communicate its flames to the tree, as accidental circumstances may determine.

Governor Phillip, on his return from this excursion, had the mortification to find that five ewes and a lamb had been killed very near the camp, and in the middle of the day. How this had happened was not known, but it was conjectured that they must have been killed by dogs belonging to the natives. The loss of any part of the stock of cattle was a serious misfortune, since it must be a considerable time before it could be replaced. Fish affords, in this place, only an uncertain resource: on some days great quantities are caught, though not sufficient to save any material part of the provisions; but at times it is very scarce. An account of the live stock at this time in the settlement is subjoined to this chapter.

The three transports bound to China, sailed the 5th, 6th, and 8th of May; and the *Supply* having been caulked, sailed on the 6th to Lord Howe Island for turtle, in hopes of giving some check to the scurvy, with which the people were still so much affected that near two hundred were incapable of work.

From the great labour which attended the clearing of the ground it proved to be impracticable to sow at present more than eight or ten acres with wheat and barley*: and it was apprehended that even this crop would suffer from the depredations of ants and field mice. In the beginning of May it was supposed, as it had been once or twice before, that the rainy season was set in; but in about a week the weather became fine again.

[* Besides what was sown by the Lieutenant Governor and other individuals, for the support of their own stock: to assist whom, the labour of the convicts was occasionally lent.]

Chapter XII.

May 1788 to June 1788

The *Supply* returns from Lord Howe Island--Some convicts assaulted by the natives--excursion of Governor Phillip to Botany Bay by Land--interview with many natives--the fourth of June celebrated--some account of the climate.

25 May 1788

On the 25th of May, the *Supply* tender returned from Lord Howe Island, but unfortunately without having been able to procure any turtle. She had met with squally weather, and had been obliged to cut away her best bower anchor, but suffered no other damage. The three transports bound for China had all appeared off the island while the *Supply* remained there.

About this time one of the convicts who, in searching for vegetables, had gone a considerable way from the camp, returned very dangerously wounded in the back. He said, that another man who had gone out for the same purpose, had been carried off by the natives in his sight, after having been wounded in the head. A shirt and hat were afterwards found, both pierced with spears, in one of the huts of the natives; but no intelligence of the man could be gained. There could be little doubt that the convicts had been the aggressors, though the man who returned strongly denied having given any kind of provocation.

30 May 1788

On the thirtieth of May, two men who had been employed in collecting rushes for thatch at some distance from the camp, were found dead. One of them had four spears in his body, one of which had pierced entirely through it: the other had not any marks of violence upon him. In this case it was clearly proved that the first injury had been offered by the unfortunate men, who paid so dearly for their dishonesty and disobedience of orders; for they had been seen with a canoe, which they had taken from one of the fishing places. These events were much regretted by Governor Phillip, as tending entirely to the frustration of the plan he had so much at heart, of conciliating the affections of the natives, and establishing a friendly intercourse with them.

As the rush-cutters tools had been carried away, the Governor thought it might be possible to discover the natives who had been concerned in this unfortunate affray; and to make them understand that the conduct of their assailants had been entirely unwarranted, and was very highly disapproved. He judged the attempt to be at least worth making, as it seemed the only way to restore that confidence which must have been interrupted by this affair. The next day, therefore, he went out with a small party, consisting altogether of twelve persons, and landed at the place where the men were killed. After traversing the country for more than twenty miles, they arrived at the north shore of Botany Bay, without having met with one of the natives.

In this place, at length, they saw about twenty canoes employed in fishing: and when the fires were made, and the party encamped to pass the night upon the beach, it was fully expected that some of those in the canoes would have joined them, but not one appeared. The next morning, though fifty canoes were drawn up on the beach, not a single person could be found belonging to them. Governor Phillip had now determined to return to Port Jackson; but as he went, keeping for some time near the sea coast, he discovered a great number of the natives, apparently more than could belong to that district, assembled at the mouth of a cave. The party was within ten yards of them before they were perceived, and the Governor had hardly time to make his people halt before numbers appeared in arms. The man who seemed to take the lead, as he advanced made signs for the English to retire, but when he saw Governor Phillip approach alone, unarmed, and in a friendly manner, he gave his spear away and met him with perfect confidence. In less than three minutes the English party found itself surrounded by two hundred and twelve men; but nothing occurred in this transaction which could in the least confirm the idea, that the natives were accustomed to act with treachery, or inclined to take any cruel advantage of superiority in numbers. The moment the offered friendship was accepted on their side, they laid down their spears and stone hatchets, and joined the party in the most amicable manner. Numbers of women and children remained at a small distance, some of whom the men afterwards brought down to receive the little articles which were offered as presents. Nothing was seen among these people which could at all prove that any of them had been engaged in the affray with the rush-cutters; and the Governor parted with them on the most friendly terms, but more convinced than ever of the necessity of treating them with a proper degree of confidence, in order to prevent disagreement. Had he gone up with all his party, or had he even hesitated a moment before he advanced himself, making the signals of friendship, a lance would probably have been thrown, after which nothing could have prevented a rencounter, which in such circumstances must have been fatal.

Here was seen the finest stream of water that had hitherto been discovered in the country, but the cove into which it runs lies very open to the sea. When the natives saw that the English were going forward towards the next cove, one of them, an old man, made signs that he might be allowed to go first. He did so, and as soon as he had ascended the hill, called out, holding up both his hands, (the usual signal of amity among these people) to signify to the natives in the next cove that they who were advancing were friends. The Governor's party did not, however, descend to that cove, but saw about forty men, so that, unless they had assembled themselves on some particular occasion, they must be more numerous in that part than had been before imagined. Governor Phillip had calculated before, from the parties he had seen, that in Botany Bay, Port Jackson, Broken Bay, and all the intermediate country, the inhabitants could not exceed one thousand five hundred. In crossing the hills at this time between Botany Bay and Port Jackson, smoke was seen on the top of Lansdown Hills, which seems to prove beyond a doubt, that the country is inhabited as far as those mountains, which are not less than fifty miles from the sea.

Further enquiries having given some reason to suppose, that one of the natives had been murdered, and several wounded, previously to the attack made upon the rush-cutters, Governor Phillip on his return, proclaimed the reward of emancipation to any convict who should discover the aggressors. This step, if it did not in this instance procure any information, seemed likely to prevent such acts of violence in future.

No very good fortune had hitherto attended the live stock belonging to the settlement, but the heaviest blow was yet to come. About this time the two bulls and four cows, belonging to Government, and to the Governor, having been left for a time by the man who was appointed to attend them, strayed into the woods, and though they were traced to some distance, never could be recovered. This was a loss which must be for some time irreparable.

4 June 1788

The fourth of June was not suffered to pass without due celebration. It was a day of remission from labour, and of general festivity throughout the settlement. At sun-rise the *Sirius* and *Supply* fired each a salute of twenty-one guns, and again at one o'clock, when the marines on shore also saluted with three vollies. At sunset the same honours were a third time repeated from the ships; large bonfires were lighted, and the whole camp afforded a scene of joy. That there might not be any exception to the happiness of this day, the four convicts who had been reprieved from death, and banished to an island in the middle of the harbour, received a full pardon, and were sent for to bear their part in the general exultation. The Governor, in his letters, with that humanity which so strongly distinguishes his character, says, he trusts that on this day there was not a single heavy heart in this part of his Majesty's dominions. His own house was the centre of conviviality to all who could be admitted to that society, nor was any thing neglected which in such a situation could mark a day of celebrity, consistently with propriety and good order. Perhaps no birth-day was ever celebrated in more places, or more remote from each other, than that of his Majesty on this day.

It was now, it seems, first generally known, that the name of Cumberland County had been given by the Governor to this part of the territory. This name had been fixed before the assembling of the first courts, for the sake of preserving regularity in the form of the public acts, in which it is usual to name the county. The boundaries fixed for Cumberland County were, on the west, Carmarthen and Lansdown Hills: on the north, the northern parts of Broken Bay; and to the southward, the southern parts of Botany Bay. Thus including completely these three principal bays, and leaving the chief place of settlement at Sydney Cove nearly in the centre.

On the 22d of June was a slight shock of an earthquake, which did not last more than two or three seconds. It was felt by most people in the camp, and by the Governor himself, who heard at the same time a noise from the southward, which he took at first for the report of guns fired at a great distance.

24 June 1788

On the 24th, a convict who had absconded on the 5th, having been guilty of a robbery, returned into the camp almost starved. He had hoped to subsist in the woods, but found it impossible. One of the natives gave him a fish, and then made signs for him to go away. He said, that afterwards he joined a party of the natives, who would have burnt him, but that with some difficulty he made his escape; and he pretended to have seen the remains of a human body actually lying on a fire, but little credit can be given to reports from such a quarter. He was of opinion that the natives were at this time in great distress for food, and said, that he had seen four of them dying in the woods, who made signs for something to eat, as if they were perishing through hunger. It is certain that very little fish could be caught at this time, and the convict seemed desirous to suggest the notion that they supplied their necessities occasionally with human flesh; but there seems to be no good foundation for such an opinion. This man was tried for his offence, pleaded guilty, and suffered with another criminal.

View in New South Wales

It was now sufficiently ascertained, that though the necessity of subsisting so long chiefly upon salt provisions, and of remaining encamped in very wet weather had produced the scurvy, and other disorders common in such circumstances, the climate itself wherein this new settlement is fixed is mild and salubrious. Heavy rains had generally attended the changes of the moon during the winter months, but there had not been any time that could properly be called a rainy season. The clearing away of the woods will of course assist the circulation of air, and continually increase the healthfulness of the place. Violent storms of thunder and lightning sometimes happened, and Governor Phillip observed the variation of his thermometer, in the shade, to amount frequently to thirty-three degrees, between eight in the morning and two in the afternoon. The report of the surgeon at this time is subjoined.

A RETURN OF SICK, ETC. JUNE 30, 1788. Marines sick in the hospital
4 Convalescents in the hospital   2 Marines sick in camp
18 Convalescents in the hospital   6 Wives and children of marines sick in the hospital   6 Total belonging to the battalion under medical treatment   36 Of marines dead from the time of embarkation to landing   1 Women dead from the time of embarkation to landing   1 Children dead from the time of embarkation to landing   1 Marines dead since landing   3 Women dead since landing   0 Children dead since landing   2 Total dead from the time of embarkation to the present date   8 Convicts sick in the hospital   20 Convalescents in the hospital   4 Convicts sick in camp   26 Convalescents in the hospital   16 Total of convicts under medical treatment   66 Male convicts dead from the time of embarkation to landing   36 Female convicts dead from the time of embarkation to landing   4 Convicts children dead from the time of embarkation to landing 5 Total   45 Male convicts dead since landing   20 Female convicts dead since landing   8 Convicts children dead since landing 8 Total dead, from the time of embarkation to the present date 81 Convicts unfit for labour, from old age, infirmities, etc.   52 JOHN WHITE, Surgeon. Sydney Cove, Port Jackson.

Chapter XIII.

June 1788 to July 1788

Particular description of Sydney Cove--Of the buildings actually erected--and of the intended town--A settlement made at the head of the harbour.

There are few things more pleasing than the contemplation of order and useful arrangement, arising gradually out of tumult and confusion; and perhaps this satisfaction cannot any where be more fully enjoyed than where a settlement of civilized people is fixing itself upon a newly discovered or savage coast. The wild appearance of land entirely untouched by cultivation, the close and perplexed growing of trees, interrupted now and then by barren spots, bare rocks, or spaces overgrown with weeds, flowers, flowering shrubs, or underwood, scattered and intermingled in the most promiscuous manner, are the first objects that present themselves; afterwards, the irregular placing of the first tents which are pitched, or huts which are erected for immediate accommodation, wherever chance presents a spot tolerably free from obstacles, or more easily cleared than the rest, with the bustle of various hands busily employed in a number of the most incongruous works, increases rather than diminishes the disorder, and produces a confusion of effect, which for a time appears inextricable, and seems to threaten an endless continuance of perplexity. But by degrees large spaces are opened, plans are formed, lines marked, and a prospect at least of future regularity is clearly discerned, and is made the more striking by the recollection of the former confusion.

Sketch of Sydney Cove

To this latter state the settlement at Sydney Cove had now at length arrived, and is so represented in the plan annexed. Lines are there traced out which distinguish the principal street of an intended town, to be terminated by the Governor's house, the main guard, and the criminal court. In some parts of this space temporary barracks at present stand, but no permanent buildings will be suffered to be placed, except in conformity to the plan laid down. Should the town be still further extended in future, the form of other streets is also traced in such a manner as to ensure a free circulation of air. The principal streets, according to this design, will be two hundred feet wide; the ground proposed for them to the southward is nearly level, and is altogether an excellent situation for buildings. It is proposed by Governor Phillip that when houses are to be built here, the grants of land shall be made with such clauses as will prevent the building of more than one house on one allotment, which is to consist of sixty feet in front, and one hundred and fifty feet in depth. These regulations will preserve a kind of uniformity in the buildings, prevent narrow streets, and exclude many inconveniences which a rapid increase of inhabitants might otherwise occasion hereafter. It has been also an object of the Governor's attention to place the public buildings in situations that will be eligible at all times, and particularly to give the storehouses and hospital sufficient space for future enlargement, should it be found necessary.

The first huts that were erected here were composed of very perishable materials, the soft wood of the cabbage palm, being only designed to afford immediate shelter. The necessity of using the wood quite green made it also the less likely to prove durable. The huts of the convicts were still more slight, being composed only of upright posts, wattled with slight twigs, and plaistered up with clay. Barracks and huts were afterwards formed of materials rather more lasting. Buildings of stone might easily have been raised, had there been any means of procuring lime for mortar. The stone which has been found is of three sorts: A fine free stone, reckoned equal in goodness to that of Portland; an indifferent kind of sand stone, or firestone; and a sort which appears to contain a mixture of iron. But neither chalk, nor any species of lime-stone has yet been discovered. In building a small house for the Governor on the eastern side of the Cove, (marked 1 in the plan) lime was made of oyster shells, collected in the neighbouring coves; but it cannot be expected that lime should be supplied in this manner for many buildings, or indeed for any of great extent. Till this difficulty shall be removed by the discovery of chalk or lime-stone, the public buildings must go on very slowly, unless care be taken to send out those articles as ballast in all the ships destined for Port Jackson. In the mean time the materials can only be laid in clay, which makes it necessary to give great thickness to the walls, and even then they are not so firm as might be wished. Good clay for bricks is found near Sydney Cove, and very good bricks have been made. The wood, from the specimens that have been received in England, appears to be good; it is heavy indeed, but fine grained, and apparently strong, and free from knots. The imperfections that were found in it at first arose probably from the want of previous seasoning.

The hospital is placed on the west side of the Cove, in a very healthful situation, entirely clear of the town; and is built in such a manner as to last for some years. On the high ground between the hospital and the town, if water can be found by sinking wells, it is the Governor's intention to erect the barracks, surrounding them with proper works. These were to have been begun as soon as the transports were cleared, and the men hutted, but the progress of work was rendered so slow by the want of an adequate number of able workmen, that it was necessary to postpone that undertaking for a time. The ground marked out for a church lies still nearer to the town, so that this edifice will form in part one side of the principal parade. The design which demanded the most immediate execution was that of a storehouse, which might be secure from the danger of fire. In a country exposed to frequent storms of thunder and lightning, it was rather an uneasy situation to have all the provisions and other necessaries lodged in wooden buildings, covered with thatch of the most combustible kind. On the point of land that forms the west side of the Cove, and on an elevated spot, a small observatory has been raised under the direction of Lieutenant Dawes, who was charged by the Board of Longitude with the care of observing the expected comet. The longitude of this observatory is ascertained to be 159° 19' 30" east from Greenwich, and the latitude 32° 52' 30" south. A small house, built by the Lieutenant Governor for himself, forms at present the corner of the parade; the principal street will be carried on at right angles with the front of this building. Instead of thatch, they now use shingles made from a tree in appearance like a fir, but producing a wood not unlike the English oak. This, though more secure than thatching, is not enough so for storehouses. For these, if slate-stone should not be found, tiles must be made of the clay which has been used for bricks. The principal farm is situated in the next cove to the east of the town, and less than half a mile from it. When the plan was drawn it contained about nine acres laid down in corn of different kinds. Later accounts speak of six acres of wheat, eight of barley, and six of other grain, as raised on the public account, and in a very promising way.

Sydney cove lies open to the north-east, and is continued in a south-west direction for near a thousand yards, gradually decreasing from the breadth of about one thousand four hundred feet, till it terminates in a point, where it receives a small stream of fresh water. The anchorage extends about two thousand feet up the cove, and has soundings in general of four fathoms near the shore, and five, six, or seven, nearer the middle of the channel. It is perfectly secure in all winds; and for a considerable way up on both sides, ships can lie almost close to the shore: nor are there, in any part of it, rocks or shallows to render the navigation dangerous. Such a situation could not fail to appear desireable to a discerning man, whose object it was to establish a settlement, which he knew must for some time depend for support on the importation of the principal necessaries of life.

It is supposed that metals of various kinds abound in the soil on which the town is placed. A convict, who had formerly been used to work in the Staffordshire lead mines, declared very positively, that the ground which they were now clearing, contains a large quantity of that ore: and copper is supposed to lie under some rocks which were blown up in sinking a cellar for the public stock of spirituous liquors. It is the opinion of the Governor himself that several metals are actually contained in the earth hereabouts, and that mines may hereafter be worked to great advantage: but at present he strongly discourages any search of this kind, very judiciously discerning, that in the present situation of his people, which requires so many exertions of a very different nature, the discovering of a mine would be the greatest evil that could befal the settlement. In some places where they dug, in making wells, they found a substance which at first was taken for a metal, but which proving perfectly refractory in a very strong and long continued

33

heat, has since been concluded to be black lead. The kind of pigment called by painters Spanish brown, is found in great abundance, and the white clay with which the natives paint themselves is still in greater plenty. The Abbe le Receveur was of opinion, that this clay, if cleared from the sand, which might easily be separated, would make excellent porcelain.

The climate at Sydney Cove is considered, on the whole, as equal to the finest in Europe. The rains are not ever of long duration, and there are seldom any fogs: the soil, though in general light, and rather sandy in this part, is full as good as usually is found so near the sea-coast. All the plants and fruit trees brought from Brasil and the Cape, which were not damaged in the passage, thrive exceedingly; and vegetables have now become plentiful, both the European sorts and such as are peculiar to this country. In the Governor's garden are excellent cauliflowers, and melons very fine of their kinds. The orange trees flourish, and the fig trees and vines are improving still more rapidly. In a climate so favourable, the cultivation of the vine may doubtless be carried to any degree of perfection; and should not other articles of commerce divert the attention of the settlers from this point, the wines of New South Wales may, perhaps, hereafter be sought with avidity, and become an indispensable part of the luxury of European tables.

The rank grass under the trees, unfortunately proved fatal to all the sheep purchased by Governor Phillip, on his own and on the public account. Those which private individuals kept close to their own tents, and fed entirely there, were preserved. Hogs and poultry not only thrive but increase very fast; black cattle will doubtless succeed as well, and it will be easy in future to secure them from straying. The horses have not met with any accident.

The last dispatches from Governor Phillip bring an account of his having sent a small detachment up to that ground at the upper end of Port Jackson, which he discovered in one of his excursions to be so highly fit for cultivation. This party consisted of a captain, two lieutenants of marines, with twenty-five non-commissioned officers and privates: about fifty convicts were added as labourers. This spot is very pleasant, and has been named by the Governor, Rose-hill. The flax-plant, which was seen at the first arrival of our people, has not been found since in any great abundance. A most ample supply of this valuable article may, however, always be obtained from Norfolk Island. Governor Phillip, when he judged the seeds to be ripe, ordered them to be collected, but at that time very few of the plants were found, and not any in the places where the greatest quantity had been seen. It is thought that the natives pull up the plant when it is in flower to make their fishing lines.

On the whole, notwithstanding the difficulties and disadvantages at first experienced, which, though great, were not more than must naturally be expected to occur in such an undertaking; notwithstanding the sicknesses which from various causes prevailed for some time among the people, the settlement at Sydney Cove wore a very promising aspect at the time when the last accounts were sent; and there can be no doubt that it will be found hereafter fully to answer every expectation which was formed when the design was projected. The scantiness of the streams of fresh water was thought at first unfavourable, but good springs have since been found by digging. The house built for Governor Phillip stands about fifty-six feet above high-water mark, and there, by sinking a well about fifteen feet in the rock, an excellent spring of pure water has been obtained.

Chapter XIV.

July 1788 to October 1788

Fish violently seized by the natives--Another expedition of the Governor--Further account of the manners and manufactures of the native inhabitants of New South Wales--Difficulty of obtaining any intercourse.

9 July 1788

On the ninth of July, an effort was made by a party of natives, which seems to indicate that they were still distressed for provisions, or that they very highly resent the incroachments made upon their fishing places. A general order had been issued to those sent out on fishing parties, to give a part of what was caught to the natives if they approached, however small the quantity taken might be; and by these means they had always been sent away apparently satisfied. But on this day, about twenty of them, armed with spears, came down to the spot where our men were fishing, and without any previous attempt to obtain their purpose by fair means, violently seized the greatest part of the fish which was in the seine. While this detachment performed this act of depredation, a much greater number stood at a small distance with their spears poized, ready to have thrown them if any resistance had been made. But the cockswain who commanded the fishing party, very prudently suffered them to take away what they chose, and they parted on good terms. This is the only instance in which these people have attempted any unprovoked act of violence, and to this they probably were driven by necessity. Since this transaction, an officer has always been sent down the harbour with the boat.

Governor Phillip went out about this time with a small party, to examine the land between Port Jackson and Broken Bay. Here were found many hundred acres of land, free from timber, and very fit for cultivation. He proceeded as far as Pitt Water, and saw several of the natives, but none of them chose to approach. When the party returned to the boats near the mouth of the harbour, about sixty of these people, men, women, and children, were assembled there. Some hours were passed with them in a peaceful and very friendly manner, but though in all this time they discovered no uneasiness, they seemed best pleased when their visitors were preparing to depart. This has always been the case, since it has been known among them that our people intend to remain on the coast. Many of the women were employed at this time in fishing, a service which is not uncommonly performed by them, the men being chiefly occupied in making canoes, spears, fish-gigs, and the other articles that constitute their small stock of necessary implements. Two women were here observed to be scarred on the shoulders like the men; this was the first instance in which they had been seen so marked.

The sailors who waited on the beach to take care of the boat saw about two hundred men assembled in two parties, who after some time drew themselves up on opposite sides, and from each party men advanced singly and threw their spears, guarding themselves at the same time with their shields. This seemed at first to be merely a kind of exercise, for the women belonging to both parties remained together on the beach; afterwards it had a more serious aspect, and the women are said to have run up and down in great agitation uttering violent shrieks. But it was not perceived that any men were killed.

As it had been supposed that many of the natives had left this part of the coast, on account of the great scarcity of fish, the different coves of the harbour were examined in one day. At this time, not more than sixty-seven canoes were counted, and about one hundred and thirty of the people were seen. But it was the season in which they make their new canoes, and large parties were known to be in the woods for that purpose.

A few days after this examination, Governor Phillip himself went again to explore the coast between Port Jackson and Botany Bay. In this journey few of the natives were seen, but new proofs were observed of their having been distressed for food. In the preceding summer they would not eat either the shark or the sting-ray, but now even coarser meat was acceptable, and indeed any thing that could afford the smallest nourishment. A young whale had just been driven upon the coast, which they were busily employed in carrying away. All that were seen at this time had large pieces of it, which appeared to have been laid upon the fire only long enough to scorch the outside. In this state they always eat their fish, never broiling it for more than a few minutes; they broil also the fern root, and another root, of which the plant is not yet known; and they usually eat together in families. Among the fruits used by them is a kind of wild fig; and they eat also the kernels of that fruit which resembles a pine-apple. The latter, when eaten by some of the French seamen, occasioned violent retchings; possibly the natives may remove the noxious qualities, by some process like those employed upon the cassada. The winter months, in which fish is very scarce upon the coast, are June, July, August, and part of September. From the beaten paths that are seen between Port Jackson and Broken Bay, and in other parts, it is thought that the natives frequently change their situation, but it has not been perceived that they make any regular migrations to the northward in the winter months, or to the south in summer.

In consequence of the very extraordinary shyness of these people since the arrival of our settlement, little addition has been made to the knowledge of their manners attained by Captain Cook: but most of his observations have been confirmed. The whole, indeed, that can be known of a people, among whom civilization and the arts of life have made so small a progress, must amount to very little. The assertion that they have no nets*, is amongst the very few that have been found erroneous. Some small nets have been brought over, the manufacture of which is very curious. The twine of which they are made, appears to be composed of the fibres of the flax plant, with very little preparation; it is very strong, heavy, and so admirably well twisted as to have the appearance of the best whipcord. Governor Phillip mentions having had lines of their manufacture, which were made from the fur of some animal, and others that appeared to be of cotton. The meshes of their nets are formed of large loops, very artificially inserted into each other, but without any knots. At a small distance they have exactly the appearance of our common nets, but when they are closely examined the peculiar mode in which the loops are managed is very remarkable. Some ladies who have inspected one of these nets lately imported, declare that it is formed exactly on the same principle as the ground of point lace, except that it has only one turn of the thread, instead of two, in every loop. This net appears to have been used either as a landing net, or for the purpose of carrying the fish when taken. They have also small hoop nets, in which they catch lobsters, and sea crayfish. Their canoes and other implements are very exactly described by Captain Cook.

Axe, Basket, and Sword

The inhabitants of New South Wales have very few ornaments, except those which are impressed upon the skin itself, or laid on in the manner of paint. The men keep their beards short, it is thought by scorching off the hair, and several of them at the first arrival of our people seemed to take great delight in being shaved. They sometimes hang in their hair the teeth of dogs, and other animals, the claws of lobsters, and several small bones, which they fasten there by means of gum; but such ornaments have never been seen upon the women. Though they have not made any attempt towards clothing themselves, they are by no means insensible of the cold, and appear very much to dislike the rain. During a shower they have been observed to cover their heads with pieces of bark, and to shiver exceedingly. Governor Phillip was convinced by these circumstances that clothing would be very acceptable to them, if they could be induced to come enough among the English to learn the use of it. He has therefore applied for a supply of frocks and jackets to distribute among them, which are to be made long and loose, and to serve for either men or women.

The bodies of these people in general smell strongly of oil, and the darkness of their colour is much increased by dirt. But though in these points they shew so little delicacy, they are not without emotions of disgust, when they meet with strong effluvia to which their organs are unaccustomed. One of them, after having touched a piece of pork, held out his finger for his companions to smell, with strong marks of distaste. Bread and meat they seldom refuse to take, but generally throw it away soon after. Fish they always accept very eagerly.

Whether they use any particular rites of burial is not yet known, but from the following account it seems evident that they burn their dead. The ground having been observed to be raised in several places, like the ruder kind of graves of the common people in our church yards, Governor Phillip caused some of these barrows to be opened. In one of them a jaw bone was found not quite consumed, but in general they contained only ashes. From the manner in which these ashes were disposed, it appeared that the body must have been laid at length, raised from the ground a few inches only, or just enough to admit a fire under it; and having been consumed in this posture, it must then have been covered lightly over with mould. Fern is usually spread upon the surface, with a few stones, to keep it from being dispersed by the wind. These graves have not been found in very great numbers, nor ever near their huts.

When the latest accounts arrived from Port Jackson, the natives still avoided all intercourse with our settlement, whether from dislike or from contempt is not perfectly clear: They think perhaps that we cannot teach them any thing of sufficient value to make them amends for our encroachments upon their fishing places. They seem to be among themselves perfectly honest, and often leave their spears and other implements upon the beach, in full confidence of finding them untouched. But the convicts too frequently carry them off, and dispose of them to vessels coming to England, though at the hazard on one side of being prosecuted for theft, and on the other for purchasing stolen goods. Injuries of this nature they generally revenge on such stragglers as they happen to meet; and perhaps have already learnt to distinguish these freebooters, by their blue and yellow jackets, as they very early did the soldiers by their red clothes. Beyond these attacks they have not yet committed any open acts of hostility, except the seizing of the fish in the instance above related. They have not attempted to annoy the settlers by setting fire to the grass, as they did when Captain Cook was on the coast; nor have they, which is more important, shown any desire to burn the crops of corn. So absolutely indispensable to the welfare of the settlement is the preservation of the grain, that an attempt of this kind must at all events be counteracted; but in no other case will any harsh measures be adopted, or any effort made to drive them to a greater distance. Conciliation is the only plan intended to be pursued: But Governor Phillip, when he last wrote, seemed to despair of getting any of them to remain among his people, long enough for either to acquire the language of the other, except by constraint. Hitherto he has been unwilling to take this method, but if it can be done in such a manner as not to create any general alarm among them, it will probably turn out to be the kindest piece of violence that could be used. Whenever it shall be practicable, by any means, to explain to them the friendly disposition of Governor Phillip and his people towards them, and to make them understand, that the men from whom they receive occasional injuries, are already a disgraced class, and liable to severe punishment for such proceedings, they will then perhaps acquire sufficient confidence in their new countrymen to mix with them, to enrich themselves with some of their implements, and to learn and adopt some of the most useful and necessary of their arts. It may, indeed, admit of a doubt whether many of the accommodations of civilized life, be not more than counterbalanced by the artificial wants to which they give birth;

but it is undeniably certain that to teach the shivering savage how to clothe his body, and to shelter himself completely from the cold and wet, and to put into the hands of men, ready to perish for one half of the year with hunger, the means of procuring constant and abundant provision, must be to confer upon them benefits of the highest value and importance.

According to the latest advices from Governor Phillip, the *Sirius* sailed for the Cape on the 2d of October, 1788, to purchase grain, flour, and other necessaries. Live stock was not to be procured by this ship, as being less wanted in the present state of the settlement, which had provisions in store for eighteen months, but not grain enough for seed, and for the support of cattle. The *Fishburn* and *Golden Grove* storeships sailed in November for England; the *Supply* was detained in Port Jackson for occasional use. At this time the officers were all in separate houses, and the whole detachment comfortably lodged, though the barracks were yet unfinished. Nothing more, that requires to be related, has yet been heard from the settlement.

REMARKS and DIRECTIONS for SAILING into PORT JACKSON, by Capt. J. HUNTER, of the *Sirius*.

In coming in with Port Jackson, you will not immediately discover where the harbour is: Steer right in for the outer points, for there is not any thing in the way but what shows itself by the sea breaking on it, except a reef on the south shore which runs off a small distance only: when you are past this reef and are a-breast the next point on the same side, you will open to the south-ward of you an extensive branch of the harbour, into which you will sail; taking care to keep the shore on either side well on board, for there is a reef which dries at low water and lies very near the mid-channel, right off the first sandy cove on the east shore; this reef is pretty broad athwart, as well as up and down the channel, and shoals very gradually: The marks for it are, the outer north point and inner south point touching, Green Point will then be on with a remarkable notch in the back land. To avoid it to the eastward, pass the inner south head a cable's length from it, and when you open any part of the sandy beach of Camp Cove, haul short in for it until you bring the inner north head and inner south head on with each other; that mark will carry you up in five and six fathom: But if you cannot weather the reef, tack and stand into Camp Cove, which shoals gradually. If you pass to the westward of the reef, steer in for Middle Cape, which is steep too, then steer up for the next point above it on the same side; when you are that length, you may take what part of the channel you please, or anchor where you like.

It flows Full and Change a quarter past eight.

Rises 4 6 Neap Tide.
Rises 6 0 Spring Tide.

Plan of Port Jackson
Chapter XV.

Some Specimens of Animals from New South Wales.

The great advantage of a scientific eye over that of the unlearned observer, in viewing the productions of nature, cannot be more strongly exemplified than by the present state of the natural history of Botany Bay, and its vicinity. The English who first visited this part of the coast, staid there only a week, but having among them persons deeply versed in the study of nature, produced an account, to which the present settlers, after a residence of near eleven months when the last dispatches were dated, have been able to add but very little of importance. The properties and relations of many objects are known to the philosopher at first sight, his enquiries after novelty are conducted with sagacity, and when he cannot describe by name what he discovers, as being yet unnamed, he can at least refer it to its proper class and genus. The observation of unskilful persons is often detailed by trivial resemblances, while it passes by the marks which are really characteristic. Governor Phillip, in one of his letters, remarking the prodigious variety of vegetable productions then before his eyes, laments, that among all the people with him there happens not to be one who has any tolerable knowledge of botany. This circumstance is perhaps less to be regretted than a deficiency in any other branch of natural knowledge. The researches of some gentlemen among the first voyagers were particularly directed to botanical discoveries, and a work which is now preparing, in a style of uncommon accuracy and elegance by one of the most illustrious of them, will probably discover that there was little left undone, even in their short stay, towards completing that branch of enquiry. Of quadrupeds the whole stock contained in the country appears to be confined to a very few species: Wolves have not been seen, though the tracks of them were so frequently thought to be detected on this coast by Captain Cook's party. Birds are numerous, but they belong in general to classes already known to naturalists; a few drawings however, and specimens of both, have been sent over. These, to gratify, as far as possible, the curiosity of those readers whose attention is particularly directed to natural history, have been engraved, and a short account of them is thrown together in this chapter. Of reptiles few have been seen that are at all curious. A large Lizard, of the Scincus kind, with the remarkable peculiarity of a small spine or horn standing near the extremity of the tail, is said to be among some specimens sent over as private presents; and also a kind of frog, whose colour is blue; but these do not in other respects differ materially from the usual form of their respective species. The ants are fully described in Captain Cook's first voyage.

QUADRUPEDS.

The **KANGUROO** has been particularly described already.

THE SPOTTED OPOSSUM.

The annexed plate represents a small animal of the opossum kind, which has not before been delineated. It is perhaps the same which is slightly described in Captain Cook's first voyage as resembling a polecat, having the back spotted with white; and is there said to be called by the natives Quoll.* The colour however is darker, being rather black than brown.

[* Hawkesw. iii. p. 222.]

Spotted Opossum

The Spotted Opossum, for so it may properly be named, is in length from the nose to the extremity of the tail about twenty-five inches, of which the tail itself takes up about nine or ten. The general colour of the animal is black, inclining to brown beneath; the neck and body spotted with irregular roundish patches of white; the ears are pretty large, and stand erect, the visage is pointed, the muzzle furnished with long slender hairs; the fore, as well as hind legs, from the knees downward, almost naked, and ash-coloured; on the fore feet are five claws, and on the hind, four and a thumb without a claw; the tail, for about an inch and an half from the root, covered with hairs of the same length as those on the body, from thence to the end with long ones not unlike that of a squirrel. The specimen from which the above account was taken, is a female, and has six teats placed in a circle, within the pouch.

Another animal of the opossum kind has been sent alive to the Rev. Dr. Hamilton, Rector of St. Martin's, Westminster, and is now living in the possession of Mr. J. Hunter. It appears to be of the same sort as that mentioned in Captain Cook's first voyage,* and that also which was found near Adventure Bay, represented in the eighth plate of Captain Cook's third voyage, and slightly described in Vol. I. p. 109 of that work: but it must be owned, that neither its form nor character is very well expressed in that plate.

[* Hawkesw. vol. iii. p. 182.]

The countenance of this animal much resembles that of a fox, but its manners approach more nearly to those of the squirrel. When disposed to sleep, or to remain inactive, it coils itself up into a round form; but when eating, or on the watch for any purpose, sits up, throwing its tail behind it. In this posture it uses its fore feet to hold any thing, and to feed itself. When irritated, it sits still more erect on the hind legs, or throws itself upon its back, making a loud and harsh noise. It feeds only on vegetable substances.

This specimen is a male. The fur is long, but close and thick; of a mixed brown or greyish colour on the back, under the belly and neck, of a yellowish white. Its length is about eighteen inches, exclusive of the tail, which is twelve inches long, and prehensile. The face is three inches in length, broad above and very pointed at the muzzle, which is furnished with long whiskers. The eyes are very large, but not fierce. On the fore feet are five claws; on the hind, three and a thumb. The teeth are two in the front of the upper jaw, and two in the lower; the upper projecting beyond the under. In the Kanguroo it is remarkable that there are four teeth in the upper jaw, opposed to two in the under. The testicles are contained in a pendulous scrotum, between the two thighs of the hind legs, as in the common opossum. The affinity of almost all the quadrupeds yet discovered on this coast to the opossum kind, in the circumstance of the pouch in which the female receives and suckles her young, seems to open a field of investigation most interesting to the naturalist: and the public will doubtless learn with pleasure, that it is the intention of the most able comparative anatomist of the age, to give a paper on this subject to the Royal Society. It cannot, therefore, be necessary at present to pursue the enquiry any farther.

THE VULPINE OPOSSUM.

This is not unlike the common fox in shape, but considerably inferior to it in respect to size, being, from the point of the nose to the setting on of the tail, only twenty-six inches; the tail itself fifteen inches: the upper parts of the body are of a grisly colour, arising from a mixture of dusky and white hairs, with rufous-yellow tinge; the head and shoulders partaking most of this last colour: round the eyes blackish: above the nostrils ten or twelve black whiskers, four inches or more in length: all the under parts of the body are of a tawny buff-colour, deepest on the throat, where the bottom of the hairs are rust-colour: the tail is of the colour of the back for about one quarter of its length, from thence to the end, black: the toes on the fore feet are five in number, the inner one placed high up: on the hind feet four toes only: with a thumb, consisting of two joints, without a claw, placed high up at the base of the inner toe. The whole foot serving the purpose of a hand, as observable in many of the opossum genus. The legs are much shorter in proportion than those of the common fox: the ears about one inch and an half in length: in the upper jaw are six cutting teeth, and four grinders, with two small canine teeth placed at an equal distance between them: in the under jaw two long cutting teeth, not unlike those of a squirrel, and four grinders to answer those in the upper jaw, but no canine teeth.--A representation of the mouth and teeth may be seen in one of the following plates.

Vulpine Opossum
NORFOLK ISLAND FLYING SQUIRREL.

Size of the American grey squirrel, and the general colour of the upper parts very nearly resembling that animal; the under parts white: from the nose to the tail runs a streak of dusky black, and another springs on each side of the head behind the nostrils, passing over the eyes and finishing behind them: ears not rising from the head: on each side of the body is a broad flap or membrane, as in other flying squirrels, which is united to both the fore and hind legs, as usual in many of this division: this membrane is black, fringed on the outer edge with white: the tail for two-thirds of the length, is of an elegant ash colour, paler than the body, from thence to the end dusky black: the toes on the fore legs are five in number; those of the hinder uncertain, as the legs behind were wanting: length from head to rump nine inches; the tail is ten inches.

Norfolk Island Flying Squirrel
BIRDS.
BLUE BELLIED PARROT. Order II. Pies. Genus V. Species XIV. Var. B. Described thus by Mr. Latham.

"The length of this beautiful parrot is fifteen inches. The bill is reddish: orbits black: head and throat dark blue, with a mixture of lighter blue feathers: back part of the head green; towards the throat yellow green: back and wings green: prime quills dusky, barred with yellow: breast red, mixed with yellow: belly of a fine blue: thighs green and yellow: tail cuneiform; the two middle feathers green; the others the same, but bright yellow on the outer edges: legs dusky. Inhabits Botany Bay in New Holland." Latham's Synopsis, vol. i. p. 213.

To this account little need be added, except that in our present specimens the parts there said to be blue are rather a bright lilac: the bill is a deep orange; and there are red spots on the back between the wings, and a few near the vent feathers.

Blue-bellied Parrot
TABUAN PARROT. Order and Genus the same. Species XVI. A Variety.

The bird here represented has been seen by Mr. Latham, and was by him referred to this species; of which however it seems a very remarkable variety: The prevalent colour of the head, neck and breast, being, instead of a deep crimson or purplish red, as in his description and plate, as well as in a fine specimen now in his own collection, a very bright scarlet: the blue mark across the lower part of the neck appears the same; but the blue feathers in the wings are entirely wanting; and the bill is not black. (See Latham's Synopsis, vol. i. p. 214.)

The specimen here delineated may be thus described.

Length twenty-four inches: bill brown, the upper mandible tinged with red: the head, neck, and all the under parts of the body a bright scarlet: the back and wings a fine green. On the lower part of the neck, between that and the back, a crescent of blue: the tail long and cuneiform, most of its feathers deep blue: the legs ash coloured: on the upper part of the wings a narrow line of lighter green.

Tabuan Parrot
PENNANTIAN PARROT. Order and Genus the same. Species, 134.

Size of the scarlet lory, length sixteen inches: the bill of a blueish horn colour; the general colour of the plumage scarlet; the base of the under mandible and the chin covered with rich blue feathers: the back black, the feathers edged with crimson: wings blue, down the middle much paler than the rest: the quills and tail black, the feathers edged outwardly with blue, and three of the outer tail feathers, from the middle to the end, of a pale hoary blue: the tail is wedge shaped, the middle feathers eight inches in length; the outermost, or shortest, only four: the bottom of the thighs blue, legs dusky, claws black.

This beautiful bird is not unfrequent about Port Jackson, and seems to correspond greatly with the Pennantian Parrot, described by Mr. Latham in the supplement to his General Synopsis of Birds, p. 61. differing in so few particulars, as to make us suppose it to differ only in sex from that species.

Pennantian Parrot
PACIFIC PAROQUET. Order and Genus the same. Species L VI. A new variety.

Mr. Latham's description is this:

"Length twelve inches, bill of a silvery blue; end black: in some, the forehead and half the crown; in others, the forehead only, of a deep crimson: behind each eye a spot of the same colour: on each side of the vent a patch of the same: the plumage in general of a dark green, palest on the under parts: the tail is cunei-form; the two middle feathers are five inches and an half in length; the outer ones two inches and an half; upper parts of it the same green with the body; beneath ash colour: the outer edge of the wings, as far as the middle of the quills, deep blue; the ends of the quills dusky: legs brown: claws black." Latham's Synopsis, vol. I. p. 252.

The variety here represented has a brown bill, tinged with red at the end, and a cap of azure blue at the back of the head, interspersed with a few small feathers of a yellowish green; the top of the wings is of a yellow hue, and there are no blue feathers in the wings.

Pacific Parrakeet
THE SACRED KING'S FISHER. Order of Birds II. Pies. Genus XXIII. Species 12.

The following description is extracted from Mr. Latham's Synopsis of Birds, vol. ii. p. 623. The specimen here represented, being the same as his fourth variety of that species marked D.

"This in size is rather less than a blackbird: the bill is black; the lower mandible yellowish at the base: head, back, wings, and tail, blue tinged with green: the under parts of the body white, extending round the middle of the neck like a collar: legs blackish."

To which account we may add, that the bill is very strong at the base, and sharp at the point; that the feathers immediately above the bill are tinged with yellow; and that the toes, as in most of this species, are three before and one behind.

Sacred Kings-fisher
SUPERB WARBLER, MALE. Birds, Order III. Passerine. Genus XLI. Warbler. Species 137. A new variety.

"The length of this beautiful species is five inches and a half: the bill black: the feathers of the head are long, and stand erect like a full crest; from the forehead to the crown they are of a bright blue; from thence to the nape, black like velvet: through the eyes from the bill, a line of black; beneath the eye springs a tuft of the same blue feathers; beneath these and on the chin, it is of a deep blue almost black, and feeling like velvet: on the ears is another patch of blue, and across the back part of the head a band of the same, (in some specimens, the patches of blue under the eye and on the ear unite together, and join with the band at the nape, as in the plate*) the whole giving the head a greater appearance of bulk than is natural: the hind part of the neck and upper parts of the body and tail, deep blue black; the under, pure white: wings, dusky; shafts of the quills chesnut: the tail, two inches and a quarter long, and cuneiform; the two outer feathers very short: legs dusky brown: claws black." Latham's Synopsis, vol. iv. p. 501.

[* Latham's Synopsis, vol. iv. pl. 53.]

The disposition of the blue is found to differ in most of the specimens. In the present variety, the whole head is enveloped in blue, which terminates in an irregularly waving line, and is continued below the eye in a broad band, edged in the same manner, and running almost to a point, as low as the bottom of the neck on each side; but there is no band continued round the neck, which, both above and below, is of the deep blue like velvet, mentioned by Mr. Latham. Some feathers of a very bright orange lie immediately under that blue, and above the wings*.

[* The Specimens from which Mr. Latham took his descriptions were met with at Van Diemen's Land, the most southern part of New Holland.]

Male Superb Warbler
SUPERB WARBLER, Female.

When Mr. Latham's Synopsis was published, the female of this species was entirely unknown; and it was conjectured by that author that the disposition of the blue might possibly mark the sexes. The female is now discovered to be entirely destitute of all the fine blue colours, both pale and dark, by which the male is adorned, except that there is a very narrow circle of azure round each eye, apparently on the skin only: all the upper feathers consist of shades of brown, and the whole throat and belly is pure white. Except from the shape and size, this bird would not be suspected at first sight to belong to the same species as the male: the epithet of superb applies very ill to the female.

Female Superb Warbler

CASPIAN TERN. Birds, Order IX. Webfooted. Genus LXXXVIII. Species I. Variety B. Mr. Latham's description is as follows.

"Length nineteen or twenty inches: bill three inches, stout and of a pale yellow: nostrils pervious: the crown of the head black; the feathers longish, and forming a kind of pensile crest at the nape; the rest of the head, neck, and under parts of the body, white: back and wings pale cinereous grey: quills grey, with the ends dusky; the inner webs, half way from the base, white: tail grey, forked; the end half of the other feathers white; the last is exceeded by the first an inch: legs black. Supposed to inhabit China; seen also, or very similar, from the Friendly Isles; also found at Hapaee, one of the Sandwich Islands." Syn. Vol. vi. p. 351.

NORFOLK ISLAND PETREL. Order IX. Web-Footed. Genus Xc.

Length sixteen inches, bill one inch and an half long, black, and very hooked at the tip: the head as far as the eyes, the chin and throat, waved, brown and dusky white: the rest of the body on the upper parts of a sooty brown, the under of a deep ash colour; the inner part of the quills, especially next the base, very pale, nearly white, and the wings, when closed, exceed the tail by about an inch: the tail is much rounded in shape, and consists of twelve feathers, of the same colour as the upper parts of the body: the legs are pale yellow, the outer toe black the whole length, the middle one half way from the tip, the webs also correspond, the outer one being black, except just at the base; and the inner one black for about one third from the end: the claws black; the spur, which serves in place of a back toe, is also black.

This inhabits Norfolk Island, and burrows in the sand like a rabbit, lying hid in the holes throughout the day, and coming out of evenings in quest of food. This bird appears to differ so very little from the dark grey Petrel of Cook's Voyage, vol. i. p. 258. that it is not improbable it may prove to be the same species. This is described in the General Synopsis of Birds, vol. vi. p. 399. under the name of Grey Petrel; as also another species, in p. 400. by the name of White-breasted Petrel, differing only in the breast from our specimen.

Norfolk Island Petrel

BRONZE-WINGED PIGEON. Order IV. Columbine. Genus XLVI.

Size of a large dove-house pigeon: general colour of the plumage ash-coloured, brown on the upper parts, the feathers margined with pale rufous; the under parts pale ash-colour, with very pale margins: the wing coverts are much the same colour as the back, but the greater ones, or lower series, have each of them a large oval spot of bronze on the outer webs near the ends, forming together, when the wings are closed, two bars of the most brilliant and beautiful bronze, changing into red, copper, and green, in different reflections of light: several of the feathers also among the other coverts have the same spots on them, but are irregularly placed: the quills are brown, with the inner webs, from the middle to the base, pale rufous; as are the sides of the body and all the under wing coverts: the tail consists of sixteen feathers; the two middle ones are brown, the others pale lead, or dove colour, with a bar of black near the tips: the bill is of a dull red: the forehead very pale, nearly white, passing a little way under the eye: the chin and throat pale grey: the legs are red.

This bird inhabits Norfolk Island; and is clearly a non-descript species.

Bronze-winged Pigeon

WHITE-FRONTED HERON. Order VII. Cloven-footed. Genus LXV.

This is little more than half the size of the common Heron: length 28 inches: the general colour of the plumage is bluish ash, inclining to lead colour: top of the head black, and a trifle crested; the forehead, sides of the head, chin, and throat white, passing downwards, and finishing in a point about the middle of the neck before: on the lower part of the neck the feathers are long and loose, and of a pale rufous cinnamon colour; all the under parts of the body also incline to this last colour, but are much paler: the quills and tail are dark lead colour, nearly black: on the back the feathers are long and narrow, and hang part of the way on the tail: the bill is four inches long, and black; but the base half of the under mandible is yellowish: the legs are formed as in other herons, of a yellowish brown colour, and the claws are black.

This bird was sent from Port Jackson in New Holland, and as it has not been noticed by any author, we consider it as a new species.

White-fronted Heron

WATTLED BEE-EATER. Order II. Pies. Genus XXVI.

The size of this bird is nearly that of a cuckow: length fourteen inches and a half: the bill one inch long, and of nearly the same shape and size as in the Poe Bird; the colour black: the general colour of the plumage is brown, palest on the under parts; most of the feathers are pointed in shape, and have a streak of white down the middle: the fore part of the head, as far as the eyes, is smooth, but the rest of the head appears full, the feathers being longer: from the gape of the bill a broad streak of silvery white passes under the eye, and beneath this, on each side of the throat, hangs a pendulous wattle, about half an inch in length, and of an orange colour: the wings, when closed, reach about one third on the tail, which is about half the length of the bird, and cuneiform in shape: both the quills and tail feathers are of a darker brown than the rest of bird, and have the tips white: the middle of the belly is yellow: the legs are of a pale brown, the hind toe very stout, and the outer toe connected to the middle one as far as the first joint.

The above inhabits New Holland; it was received from Port Jackson, and is no doubt a non-descript species.

Wattled Bee-eater
PSITTACEOUS HORNBILL. Order II. Pies. Genus VIII.

The bird is about the size of a crow: the total length two feet three inches: the bill is large, stout at the base, much curved at the point, and channelled on the sides; the colour pale brown, inclining to yellow near the end: the nostrils are quite at the base, and are surrounded with a red skin, as is the eye also, on the upper part: the head, neck, and under parts of the body are pale blue-grey; the upper parts of the body, wings, and tail, ash colour; and most of the feathers are tipt with dusky black, forming bars of that colour across the wings: the wings, when closed, reach to near three-quarters of the length of the tail: the tail itself is long, and cuneiform, the two middle feathers measuring eleven inches, and the outer one on each side little more than seven; a bar of black crosses the whole near the end, and the tips of all the feathers are white: the legs are short and scaly, and the toes placed two forwards, and two backwards, as in those of the toucan or parrot genus: the colour of legs and claws black.*

[* Mr. Latham, who has been kind enough to give his sentiments on this occasion, is of opinion that this bird does not strictly belong to any of the present established genera. The make indeed is altogether that of an hornbill, and the edges of the mandible are smooth, but the toes being placed two forwards and two backwards, seem to rank it with the Parrots or Toucans; and it has been unlucky that in the specimen from which the description was taken, the tongue was wanting, which might in a great measure have determined the point: but the inducement for placing it with the hornbills has had the greater weight, as not a single species of the toucan tribe has yet been met with in that part of the world.]

This bird was killed at Port Jackson, and we believe it to be hitherto non-descript.

Psittaceous Hornbill

Such is the account of the birds of which drawings or specimens have been obtained from Port Jackson or from Norfolk Island. Wild ducks, teal, quails, and other common species are numerous in both places, and the variety, as well as number of the small birds is considerable. Birds of the Cassowary or Emu kind have very frequently been seen; but they are so shy, and run so swiftly, that only one has yet been killed. That bird was shot near the camp, while Governor Phillip was absent on his first expedition to Broken Bay, and was thought by him to differ materially both from the ostrich and cassowary; the skin was sent over, but at the time when this sheet was printed off, had not been stuffed, or put into form. Should it, on examination, exhibit any remarkable peculiarities, we shall endeavour to obtain a description of it, to subjoin at the conclusion of this volume.

Since stating the dimensions of the kanguroo, in page 106, Lord Sydney has received from Governor Phillip, a male of a much larger size, which measures as follows.

	f. in.	Length from the point of the nose to the end of the tail, 8	5	Length of the tail,	3	1 --	head,		
0	11 --	fore legs,		2	0 --	hind legs		3	7
Circumference of the fore part by the legs,	1	9 ----	lower parts --						
4	5 Round the thicker part of the tail, which gradually tapers to the end.								
1	1								

The above is the largest kanguroo that has yet been seen, and there is every reason to believe that even this had not nearly attained its full growth.

Lieutenant Shortland describes them as feeding in herds of about thirty or forty, and assures us, that one is always observed to be apparently upon the watch, at a distance from the rest.

42

These artificers were employed on the representation of the Lieutenant-Governor to Governor Phillip, that it was impossible to erect the barracks necessary for the officers and men of the detachment, without employing such artificers for that purpose as could be found among themselves. It was at the same time represented, that these men could not properly be retained at such work, unless they were to be paid in the customary manner of paying all troops employed on extra works for the public service: and more especially, as it was known that the artificers taken from the ships of war and transports were to be paid for all work done on shore.

Governor Phillip agreed entirely as to the necessity of employing the artificers, and with respect to their pay, had no doubt that the matter must be decided by custom: In consequence of which he issued an order for that purpose on the 17th of May, 1788.

No. III.

The Right Hon. the Lords Commissioners of the Admiralty, in a letter, dated the 8th of October, 1786, addressed to the commanding officers of each division of the marines, directed them to signify to such marines as would make a voluntary tender of their service for Botany Bay, that they should at the expiration of their station of three years be entitled to their discharge on their return to England, provided their good behaviour during this service should have merited such marks of favour: Or that, if they preferred it, they should at the time of relief be discharged in New South Wales, and permitted to settle there. In consequence of this, at the date of the following paper, the question was put by the Lieutenant Governor to all the officers and men, whether they chose to remain in the country, either as soldiers or settlers. Before this question was asked, Major Ross applied to Governor Phillip to know what encouragement Government held out to those who should wish to remain in either capacity. To this application it was answered by the Governor, that the proper instructions and authorities for giving every reasonable encouragement to such of the military and others as should be desirous to remain in New South Wales, and for making grants of land, were to be sent from England as soon as Government being sufficiently informed of the actual state of the country, and the quality of the soil, at and near the settlement, could determine what was the most eligible mode of granting the lands.

Those documents having been received, the amplest powers are now to be sent out to Governor Phillip, that he may make such grants and give such encouragement as may be proportioned to the merits of those who apply, and satisfactory to every individual.

The following list exhibits the result of the question put by the Lieutenant Governor to the officers and men of the marines, concerning their desire to return, or to remain in New South Wales.

LIST of such OFFICERS, NON-COMMISSIONED OFFICERS, DRUMMERS, and PRIVATES, as are desirous of remaining in this Country, after the time when their Lordships the Commissioners of the Admiralty intended to relieve the Detachment, as expressed in their Letter of the 8th October, 1788.

NEW SOUTH WALES, 1st October, 1788.

Names and quality. Desirous of remaining in this country.

Watkin Tench, Capt. Lieutenant, as a soldier for one tour more of three years.

George Johnstone, First Lieutenant, having been so short a time in this country, cannot determine whether he would wish to remain or not, as to settling can say nothing.

John Johnstone, ditto, having been so short a time in this country, cannot determine whether he would wish to remain another tour or not, as to settling can say nothing, till he knows on what terms.

James Maitland Shairp, ditto, being so short a time in the country, he cannot yet judge whether he would wish to remain or not another tour, as to settling, until he knows the terms and nature of the grants, cannot determine.

William Dawes, Second Lieutenant, as a soldier for one tour more of three years.

William Baker, Serjeant, as a soldier.

George Flemming, private, as a soldier for three years more.

Isaac Tarr, ditto, as a settler.

James Manning, as a soldier.

All the officers, non-commissioned officers, drummers, and private men of the detachment, whose names are not expressed in the above list, wish to return to England, at the time proposed by their Lordship's letter of the 8th October, 1786, or as soon after as their Lordships may find it convenient.

R. ROSS, MAJOR.

No. IV.
AN ACCOUNT OF PROVISIONS REMAINING IN HIS MAJESTY'S STORES, AT SYDNEY COVE, NEW SOUTH WALES, 30TH SEPTEMBER, 1788.

Flour, 414,176 pounds, is 62 weeks ration. Rice, 51,330 -- -- 15 -- Beef, 127,608 -- -- 43 -- Pork, 214,344 -- -- 128 -- Pease, 2,305 bushels, -- 58 -- Butter, 15,450 pounds, -- 49 -- Number of Persons victualled. Men, 698. Women, 193. Children, 42. Provisions at Norfolk Island, twenty months. Number of Persons victualled. Men, 44. Women, 16. ANDREW MILLER, Commissary.

No. V.

Return of Sick, September 27th, 1788. Marines sick in hospital 4 ---- camp 21 Marine women and children in camp 5 Deaths since last return 0 Total belonging to the battalion under medical treatment 30 Male convicts sick 62 Female ditto and children 31 Total of convicts under medical treatment 93 Male convicts dead since the last report of June 30 6 Female convicts ditto since ditto 4 Total convicts dead since ditto 10 Convicts unserviceable from old age, infirmities, etc. 53

Chapter XVII.

Nautical directions, and other detached remarks, by Lieutenant Ball, concerning Rio de Janeiro, Norfolk Island, Ball Pyramid, and Lord Howe Island.

Some notice has already been taken in the preceding sheets of Rio de Janeiro, Norfolk Isle, and Lord Howe Isle; but since they were committed to the press, the following particulars respecting those places have very obligingly been communicated to the editor, by Lieutenant Henry Lidgbird Ball. As these remarks are the result of minute observation, they cannot fail of being useful and interesting to the seafaring reader, which, it is presumed, will be a sufficient apology for giving them a place here.

There is no danger in going up the harbour to Rio de Janeiro but what may easily be seen. The course up the harbour is north-west by north; you anchor before the town in seventeen fathoms water, over a muddy bottom; the middle of the town bearing west by north, west, or west by south, about a mile and an half distant from the watering place, and the Fort Saint Cruz bearing south-east. No pilot is necessary; the soundings a-breast of St. Cruz Fort are twenty-two fathoms, and shoal gradually to seventeen fathoms, where the ships moored a-breast of the town. The tide flows two hours and thirty minutes at full and change, and rises in general about eight feet. In going into the harbour, it is necessary to keep the starboard shore best aboard, as the tide sets on the other side, till you get nearly a-breast of St. Cruz Fort, and in that situation you must be on your guard, if going in with the flood, as the passage is narrow: and there are whirlpools in many places, which will take all command from the rudder. Water is procured at a pipe, by which it is conveyed from a fountain situated in the large square near the principal landing place, which is opposite the palace. This pipe is continued down to the waterside, and you fill your casks in boats: the water is so plentiful, that a fleet might be supplied in a short time.

Bullocks, sheep, and Portugal wine, may be had here in plenty; there is also an excellent market for poultry and vegetables every day; in short, every refreshment that is necessary for a fleet may be procured in great abundance, and very cheap.

The whole harbour, as well as the town, is defended by a number of strong fortifications; and as far as Lieutenant Ball had an opportunity of examining the harbour, the draft of it published in the East India chart is very true, the soundings right, and the bearings very accurate.

Their trade is chiefly to Portugal, and consists of bullion, indigo, sugar, rum, tobacco, brazil wood, whale-oil, whale bone, spermaceti, etc. and of late years diamonds and many other valuable commodities.

In approaching Norfolk Island there is no danger: Lieut. Ball anchored in nineteen fathoms, over a bottom of coarse sand and coral, the north-east end of the island bearing west south-west quarter west; the easternmost rocks east south-east, about a mile distant from the nearest shore: at this place Capt. Cook landed. Ships have anchored also at south end of the isle in twenty-two fathoms, the westernmost point of Phillip Isle south south-east, the body of Nepean's Isle east north-east half east, and the south point of Norfolk Isle north-east by east. They anchored again in eighteen fathoms, over a bottom of sand and coral, the west point of Phillip Isle bearing south, the easternmost point of it south south-east half east, and the south point of Norfolk Isle north-east. The pine trees on this island are of an immense size, measuring from twenty to twenty-seven and even thirty feet in girth, and so tall that it was not easy to form any exact judgment of their height. This place affords vast numbers of cabbage trees, and amazing quantities of fish may be procured on the banks that lie on the west side of the small island; those they got on board the *Supply* were of the snapper kind, and very good, yet they were caught in such abundance that many of the people were as much satiated with them as the sailors are with cod on the banks of Newfoundland.

The only places where it was found practicable to land was a-breast of their first station (which is the place described by Captain Cook, and where the people landed with the utmost difficulty,) and at Sydney Bay on the south end of the isle, the outer breaker off the westernmost point in sight bearing north-west by west half west.

Map and View of Lord Howe Island

Lord Howe Island was discovered by Lieutenant Henry Lidgbird Ball, Commander of his Majesty's tender *Supply*, on the 17th February, 1788, and was so named by him, in honour of the Right Honourable Lord Howe. At the same time he observed a remarkably high pyramidical rock at a considerable distance from the island, which has been named Ball's Pyramid; from a correct drawing of this rock and others near it, the annexed engraving was taken.

Ball's Pyramid

There is no danger in approaching Lord Howe island, the *Supply* anchored there in thirteen fathoms, sand and coral; but there lies about four miles from the south-west part of the pyramid, a dangerous rock, which shows itself a little above the surface of the water, and appears not to be larger than a boat. Lieutenant Ball had no opportunity of examining whether there is a safe passage between them or not. The island is in the form of a crescent, the convex side towards the north-east. Two points at first supposed to be separate islands, proved to be high mountains on its south-west end, the southernmost of which was named Mount Gower, and the other Mount Lidgbird; between these mountains there is a very deep valley, which obtained the name of Erskine Valley; the south-east point was called Point King, and the north-west point, Point Phillip. The land between these two points forms the concave side of the island facing the south-west, and is lined with a sandy beach, which is guarded against the sea by a reef of coral rock, at the distance of half a mile from the beach, through which there are several small openings for boats; but it is to be regretted that the depth of water within the reef no where exceeds four feet. They found no fresh water on the island, but it abounds with cabbage-palms, mangrove and manchineal trees, even up to to the summits of the mountains. No vegetables were to be seen. On the shore there are plenty of ganets, and a land-fowl, of a dusky brown colour, with a bill about four inches long, and feet like those of a chicken; these proved remarkably fat, and were very good food; but we have no further account of them. There are also many very large pigeons, and the white birds resembling the Guinea fowl, which were found at Norfolk Island, were seen here also in great numbers. The bill of this bird is red, and very strong, thick, and sharp-pointed. Innumerable quantities of exceeding fine turtle frequent this place in the summer season, but at the approach of winter they all go to the northward. There was not the least difficulty in taking them. The sailors likewise caught plenty of fish with a hook and line.

Lieutenant Shortland
Chapter XVIII.

July 1788 to August 1788

Concise account of Lieutenant Shortland--His various services--Appointed agent to the transports sent to New South Wales--Ordered by Governor Phillip to England, by Batavia--Journal of his voyage--New discoveries.

We have been induced to subjoin in this place a concise account of Lieutenant Shortland, as well because his experience as an officer has been great, as from the consideration that his journal has been deemed, by those who best know its value, of very serious importance.

Lieutenant John Shortland very early in life had a strong predilection for the Navy, and in 1755, at the age of sixteen, he entered into his Majesty's service, on board the Anson, a sixty gun ship, which went out in the fleet under the command of Admiral Boscawen. On the Banks of Newfoundland this fleet fell in with, and took the Alcide and Ly's, two French ships, of seventy-four guns. On his return from this expedition, he went on board the Culloden, a seventy-four gun ship, and was in the fleet under Admiral Byng, off Minorca. Shortly afterwards, he went into the Hampton Court, commanded by Capt. Harvey, in which ship he was present at the taking of the Foudroyant and Arpè. On his arrival in England, he went on board the Vanguard, Commodore Swanton, to the West Indies, in the fleet under Admiral Rodney, and was present at the reduction of Martinique, the Grenades, and the other islands which were then captured. In 1763, he was promoted to the rank of Lieutenant by Admiral Swanton; since which period he has always been employed in active and important services. During the late war, and for some time afterwards, he was chiefly employed in going to and from America, except in the year 1782, when he was appointed to command the transports with the 97th regiment on board, destined for the relief of Gibraltar, under convoy of his Majesty's ships Cerberus and Apollo: he was not only successful in getting all the transports in safe, but he also landed the men without any loss.

On Lieutenant Shortland's return home from this service, in endeavouring to get through the Gut of Gibraltar in the night, he was chased by a squadron of Spanish frigates, who took three of the transports in company, but he was so fortunate as to escape in the Betsey transport, and arrived safe in England, without either loss or damage. In the year 1786, he was appointed Agent to the transports sent by Government to New South Wales, at which place he arrived in January, 1788. After remaining six months at the new settlement at Port Jackson, he was ordered to England by way of Batavia, by his Excellency Governor Phillip, who honoured him with the official dispatches for Government, and he arrived in England on the 29th of May, 1789.

This summary recapitulation of Mr. Shortland's services sufficiently points out his merit and ability as an experienced seaman, without any further elogium; which, it were were wanted, might be abundantly supplied from the subsequent account of his passage from Port Jackson to Batavia.

The *Alexander*, the *Friendship*, the *Prince of Wales*, and the *Borrowdale*, were got ready in the beginning of July, 1788, to sail for England, under the care and conduct of Lieutenant Shortland; at which time Governor Phillip took the opinions of the masters of those transports concerning their route. The season was thought to be too far advanced for them to attempt the southern course, by Van Diemen's Land; and the passage by Cape Horn was objected to by the Governor. It was therefore agreed unanimously that they should go to the northward, either through Endeavour Straits, or round New Guinea. Unfortunately the ships were ill prepared to encounter the difficulties, which were to be expected in every mode of return; their complement of men was small, only six to an hundred tons, officers included; they were without a surgeon, and unprovided with those articles which have been found essential to the preservation of health in long voyages, such as bore-cole, sour-crout, portable soup, and the other antiseptics recommended by the Royal Society. It cannot therefore be wondered, though it must be deeply regretted, that the sailors should have suffered so dreadfully from the scurvy, in the length of time necessary for exploring a passage through an unknown sea perplexed with islands, where they were destitute of assistance from charts, or observations of former navigators; and were not fortunate enough to obtain a supply of salutary refreshments.

14 July 1788

Lieutenant Shortland, in the *Alexander* transport, sailed out of the harbour of Port Jackson, on Monday, July 14, 1788, directing his course to the east-north-east, with intention to touch at Lord Howe Island, and there to appoint each ship a place of rendezvous in case of separation. This necessary step, which ought to have been previously taken, had been prevented by the hurry of preparation; the *Alexander* not having been able to join the other transports till the evening before their departure. Even then, the boats, booms, and spare anchors, were stowed loose between decks, in a manner which must have produced the most dangerous consequences, had the ship been exposed in that condition to the heavy sea which it was likely she would meet with off the shore. To the very last moment, therefore, the men and officers were most busily employed in providing against this danger; and as soon as the weather appeared tolerably favourable for working out of the harbour, Lieutenant Shortland made the signal to the masters of the other transports to get under way, without waiting for his ship. When the transports had cleared the harbour they were obliged to carry a press of sail in order to get off the coast, the vessels being very light, and a powerful swell then setting in upon the shore. The wind was at the same time strong from the south-east, and continued so for two days, with the same heavy swell, which made it very difficult to keep the ships off shore.

Chart of the Track of the *Alexander*

16 July 1788

At eight, A. M. on the 16th of July, the rocks off the entrance of Port Stephens bore north-west by west distant three leagues. Lieutenant Shortland very much regretted that this place had not been surveyed; had it been known to afford safe anchorage, it would have been much more prudent to put in there and wait for a change of wind, than to attempt keeping the sea in circumstances so very unfavourable, with ships so little calculated to run along a great extent of lee shore. This day the *Prince of Wales* being two or three miles to the leeward, the signal was made for her to tack into the fleet. At nine in the evening the wind coming to the east-south-east, Lieutenant Shortland fired a gun, and made the signal to veer ship and sail on the other tack. At this time the *Prince of Wales* was about five miles on the lee bow of the *Alexander*, and the *Borrowdale* and*Friendship* close in company; but by twelve at midnight the *Friendship* only was in sight. At two, the wind shifting again to the south-south-east, the signal was once more made to veer ship, and change the tack, as lying off east would clear the coast; a strong current setting to the southward.

19 July 1788

Lieutenant Shortland, having now lost sight of the *Prince of Wales* and*Borrowdale*, was fully determined to go to Lord Howe Island to wait a day or two for them, expecting that they might probably touch there with similar intentions. On the 19th, therefore, he steered a direct course for that island, with a strong gale at south-west, but as this wind, which was exactly favourable to the intended course of the voyage, and made the anchoring place off Lord Howe Island a lee shore, continued unvaried, and blew very hard on the 20th, it appeared best to relinquish the design of calling there. At two in the afternoon, therefore, Lieutenant Shortland again altered his course and sailed north-east by north. The *Prince of Wales* and *Borrowdale*transports, were seen no more throughout the voyage, and it has since been known that they took another course; but the *Friendship* continued close in company with the *Alexander*. About noon this day, the men at the mast head discovered a very extensive shoal on the larboard beam, bearing from north by west to north by south, distant between two and three leagues. It trended north by east and south by west, and was judged to be in length about three leagues and a half. The breadth could not be ascertained, for, while the ship ran along it, the sand bank was seen to extend as far as the eye could discern. It lies in latitude 29°. 20'. south, and in longitude 158°. 48'. east, and was named by Lieutenant Shortland, Middleton Shoals.

21 July 1788

At ten in the morning, on Monday July 21, the master of the *Friendship*went on board the *Alexander*, and Carteret's harbour in New Ireland, was appointed by Lieutenant Shortland as the place of rendezvous. The same day, at half past five in the afternoon, land was discovered, bearing from south-west by west, to west half south, at the distance of about eight leagues. It trended to the north-north-west, and was about six or seven leagues in length, the land very high, with a remarkable peak, which bore south-south-west. This island was now named Sir Charles Middleton's Island: It lies in latitude 28°. 10. south, and in longitude 159°. 50. east. Lieutenant Shortland thinks it probable that the reef seen on the preceding day may be connected with this island, as it trended in a right direction for it; but it must, in that case, be of very great extent. The island was still in sight on the morning of the 22d.

24 July 1788

On Thursday July 24th, they had an accurate observation of the sun and moon to determine the longitude, and found the effect of a current to have been so great as to set the ship two degrees of longitude to the eastward of the dead reckoning. The longitude of Sir Charles Middleton's Island must therefore be corrected by that observation, and placed considerably further to the east. The latitude may be depended upon, as the bearing was observed when the sun was on the meridian.

27 July 1788

Many land birds being seen on the 27th and 28th, when the ship was by reckoning and observation near the north-west end of New Caledonia, Lieutenant Shortland very reasonably concluded that he must have passed very close to that land, though it did not happen to be discerned: probably it is low at that extremity.

31 July 1788

At noon, on Thursday the 31st, land was discovered, bearing from north half west to east-north-east, and distant about five or six leagues. As the ship was now in latitude 10°. 52'. south, Lieutenant Shortland at first conjectured it might be Egmont Island, which was seen by Capt. Carteret, notwithstanding a considerable difference in longitude, which might be accounted for from the effect of currents, as they had been for some time very strong. The longitude laid down by Captain Carteret was 164°. 49'. east; that of the *Alexander* at this time about 161°. 11'. It proved however that the difference was real, and that this was another island. Lieutenant Shortland now kept a north-west course, in which direction the land trended. He ran along the coast about six or seven leagues, and found it formed into an island by two points, the south-east of which he called Cape Sydney, the north-west, Cape Phillip. Having passed this point, he continued steering in a north-west direction till about seven o'clock the same afternoon, when the men who were reefing the top-sails for the night, discovered land bearing exactly in the ship's course. On receiving this intelligence he immediately brought to, with the ship's head off from the land, and gave a signal for the *Friendship* to do the same. They lay to all night, and the next morning were surprised with the sight of a most mountainous coast, bearing from north-east by east to west-north-west, about five or six leagues distant. This proved sufficiently that the land

47

seen the preceding day could not be Egmont Island, and Lieutenant Shortland was inclined to think that this was united to it. At six in the morning he bore away west by north, and west by north half north, as the land trended, running along the shore at five or six leagues distance. The most eastern point of this land he called Cape Henslow, the most western which was then in sight, Cape Hunter. Between these two points the land is very singularly mountainous, the summits of the mountains rising among the clouds to a prodigious height. It may be known by one summit more elevated than the rest, which, from being discovered on the first of August, was named Mount Lammas, and is thought in height to equal, if not to exceed the Peak of Teneriffe. This day the latitude was by observation 9°. 58'. south, and the longitude 160°. 21'. east. More land still continued to open to the west-north-west, and the same course was therefore kept at an equal distance from the shore till three in the afternoon, when the water appearing suddenly of a different colour, they brought to, and sounded, but found no ground at 120 fathoms. At four, a part of the land which had the appearance of a harbour, bore north-north-east distant seven leagues. The land still continued mountainous, and at six o'clock bore from north-east to north-west by west. The furthest land then in sight appeared to be at the distance of about thirteen or fourteen leagues, and was named Cape Marsh. At half past six the ships were brought to, and lay to for the night, the weather being very squally, with violent thunder, lightning, and rain.

2 August 1788

Soon after five in the morning of August the 2d, the ships made sail again, and bore away west by north, but the weather being hazy, no land was then in sight; many flying fish were seen at this time. At eleven, there being a prospect of clearer weather, Lieutenant Shortland endeavoured to make the land again. At noon the latitude was, by observation, 9°. 40'. south, and the longitude 158°. 42'. east. Lieutenant Shortland continued to steer north-west to discover whether he had reached the utmost extent of the land, and at eight in the evening spoke to the *Friendship*, and told the master that he intended to bring to at nine.

3 August 1788

At three in the morning, on Sunday August 3, land was discovered bearing from north-north-east to north-west, on which the ships stood off again with a light air of wind. At six, the land in sight appeared like several islands, and an endeavour was made to pass between them to the north, but on approaching sufficiently near, it was discovered that all these points were joined together by a low neck of land covered with trees. As the land rose in nine roundish points, which seamen call hummocks, this place was named Nine Hummock Bay. At noon on this day, the ship then standing to the south-west, in latitude 8°. 55'. south, and longitude 158°. 14'. east, the extreme points of land bore from east by north to west, when Lieutenant Shortland named the western point Cape Nepean, and the eastern Cape Pitt. The intermediate land may, he says, easily be known by the nine hummocks, and the exact resemblance they bear to islands when seen from the distance of five or six leagues. They had now light airs and calm weather, but at two in the afternoon a breeze sprung up from the eastward, and at four Cape Nepean bore north-west, half west, distant five or six leagues. At six the *Alexander* shortened sail, and stood off and on for the night under double reefed top-sails, Lieutenant Shortland imagining that he had reached the utmost extent of this land. At five, on Monday morning, the 4th of August, he made sail again, and at six a bluff point of the island bore north-north-west, distant five or six leagues: this he called Point Pleasant. At noon the latitude was by observation 8°. 54'. south, the longitude 154°. 44'. east. Point Pleasant then bore east by north; at four, the most western point of land in sight, which was then supposed to be the extreme point of the island, but proved not to be so, bore north-west by north, distant four or five leagues. From this mistake it was named Cape Deception.

Under the persuasion that he had reached the extremity of the land, but desirous to ascertain that point, Lieutenant Shortland kept the ships standing under an easy sail all night. Some islands lying close to Cape Deception, and seeming to form a good harbour, were called Hammond's Isles. At day light on the 5th of August, land was again discovered, bearing from east north-east to west by north half north, and forming a very deep bay. This land appeared in six hummocks, like islands, but was joined by a low neck of sand. Not knowing how far it might trend to the north-west, Lieutenant Shortland stood out to the south. At eleven o'clock, the longitude was observed to be 157° 30' east; and at noon the latitude was also determined by observation to be 8° 44' south. At the same time, Cape Deception bore north-east four or five leagues distant; and two remarkable hills, from their similiarity called the Two Brothers, forming the most western point then in view, bore north-west half north, distant ten leagues. At three in the afternoon, they bore away for the two Brothers, which at six bore north-west by north, distant seven leagues. At eight, the ships lay to for the night.

6 August 1788

48

At five o'clock in the morning of Wednesday, August 6th, they made sail again to the north-west; and at eight discerned a rock which had exactly the appearance of a ship under sail, with her top-gallant sails flying. So strongly were all the *Alexander*'s people prepossessed with this imagination, that the private signal was made, under the supposition that it might be either the *Boussole* or *Astrolabe*, or one of the two transports which had parted from them on the coast of New South Wales. Nor was the mistake detected till they approached it within three or four miles. This rock bore from the Two Brothers south south-west, distant one league.

Between ten and eleven, some canoes were seen with Indians in them, who came close up to the ship without any visible apprehension. Ropes were thrown to them over the stern, of which they took hold, and suffered the ship to tow them along; in this situation they willingly exchanged a kind of rings which they wore on their arms, small rings of bone, and beads of their own manufacture, for nails, beads, and other trifles, giving however a manifest preference to whatever was made of iron. Gimlets were most acceptable, but they were also pleased with nails, and pieces of iron hoops. They dealt very fairly, not betraying the least desire to steal or to defraud. But though they so readily suffered themselves to be towed after the ship, they could not by any means be prevailed upon to go along side, and whenever an attempt was made to haul up a canoe by one of the ropes, the men in it immediately disengaged themselves from that rope, and took hold of another. At the same time they appeared extremely desirous that our people should anchor on the coast, and go ashore with them; and, by way of enticement, held up the rind of an orange or lemon, the feathers of tame fowls, and other things, signifying that they might be procured on shore. They presented also to Lieutenant Shortland, a fruit, which he conceived to be the bread-fruit; it was about the size of a small cocoa-nut, brown on the outside and white within, and contained a kind of soft pithy substance which stuck between the teeth, and was rather troublesome to chew, besides three or four kernels not unlike chesnuts, but very white. The leaves of the plantain served the Indians to make boxes or small cases, of which every man had one to contain his small rings and beads. At noon a point of land which runs from the Two Brothers, and was now named Cape Satisfaction, bore north north-east; and the rock which had been mistaken for a ship was called the Eddystone, and bore north by west, distant four leagues. The Eddystone bears from Cape Satisfaction south south-west, distant two leagues. As the land from Cape Satisfaction began to trend northward, Lieutenant Shortland again entertained hopes of finding a passage.

It was understood from the natives that they called the island from which they came, Simboo; for whenever an attempt was made to put that question to them, they pointed to the land near Cape Satisfaction, and uttered that word. Of these men, Lieutenant Shortland remarks, that they were remarkably stout and well built, from which appearance he very judiciously drew a favourable conclusion with respect to the goodness and plenty of their food. Their superiority over the New Hollanders in size and strength, he says, was very striking. Their canoes, which contained from six to fourteen men, seemed to be well put together, the bows and stems very lofty, carved with various figures, and stained with a kind of red paint; in a word, they were to all appearance formed exactly upon the same model and construction as those of Otaheite. The ornaments worn by the inhabitants of Simboo were large rings of a white bone, one or more of which every man had upon his wrist, and a shell with a feather, which was tied upon the head. Lieutenant Shortland was desirous to purchase one of their lances, but could not obtain it. About two in the afternoon his visitors, finding perhaps that they had followed the ship as far as they could venture to trust themselves, left him, and made immediately for the shore. From what was seen in the possession of these people, there can be no doubt that their land produces cocoa-nuts, bread-fruit, bananas, and most other vegetables of the Society and Friendly Isles. Nor was it without the greatest regret that Lieutenant Shortland declined the invitations of the natives, and proceeded without touching for refreshments, which doubtless might have been obtained in plenty; but the length and uncertainty of his passage seemed to forbid the least delay; nor was it at this time foreseen how much superior to every other consideration the acquirement of a wholesome change of diet would be found. The bay from which these men had come he named Indian Bay. At three P. M. the longitude was, by lunar observation, 156° 55' east; and at six the furthest land in sight bore north, Cape Satisfaction east by south half east, and the body of the land north-east, distant five or six leagues. The furthest point of land north was named Cape Middleton.

7 August 1788

After lying to in the night, the ships made sail again at four in the morning of August 7th, and bore away to the north by west. At five, they saw the land which they had left the preceding night, and six or more small islands bearing from north-east to west. These were called the Treasury Isles; they are moderately high and seemed to be well clothed with trees and herbage. At noon, the latitude was by observation 7° 24' south, the longitude 156° 30' east; and the north-

49

west extremity of the land then in sight, which was named Cape Allen, bore east by south, distant six leagues: Cape Middleton, south-east, distant eight leagues. Off Cape Allen lies a small island, to which the name of Wallis Island was given. At six in the afternoon the extremes of the islands in sight bore from north-east by east to west by north; and the entrance between two islands, which formed a passage or strait, bore north by east, distant five or six leagues.

The *Alexander* and the *Friendship* had now run from the latitude of 10° 44' south, and longitude 161° 30' east, to the latitude of 7° 10' south, and longitude 156° 50' east, the whole way nearly in sight of land. As, therefore, proceeding westward, to the south of the next land, might have entangled them with New Guinea, Lieutenant Shortland determined to try the passage which was now before him; and being very well convinced, before it was dark, that the way was clear, kept under a commanding sail all night. At ten o'clock in the evening, the *Alexander* was nearly a-breast of the two points that form the passage, and the soundings were very irregular, from ten to thirty fathoms, on a soft, sandy bottom: the anchors were therefore cleared, that they might immediately be dropped if it should prove necessary.

8 August 1788

At two in the morning of August the 8th, a strong ripple of a current was very plainly to be perceived; and by five the ship had nearly cleared the straits. She had then the following bearings: Cape *Alexander*, south-east; some islands and rocks that lie off the most western island of those which form the straits, west by south; and the remotest point in sight to the north-westward, north-west by north, distant fourteen or fifteen leagues. This point is remarkably high and forms the centre of a large body of land, between the first and last point of the straits on the western side, which were called Cape *Friendship*, and Cape Le Cras.

These straits Lieutenant Shortland judged to be between four and five leagues in length, and about seven or eight miles broad, running in a north-west direction; and, conceiving himself to be the first navigator who had sailed through them, he ventured to give them the name of Shortland's Straits. On comparing his account with the narrative of M. Bougainville, which he had not then by him, there seems to be reason to suspect that this is the same passage through which that navigator sailed at the latter end of June, 1768; and that the island supposed to be called Simboo, is the same which was then named Choiseul Island. To corroborate this suspicion, M. Bougainville's description of the canoes and persons of the natives agrees entirely, as far as it goes, with that given by Mr. Shortland*. A small difference in longitude affords the chief reason for doubting the identity of the passage, which, should it be proved, will not detract at all from the merit of the latter navigator, who proceeded entirely by his own attention and sagacity, in a sea unknown to himself and those who were with him, which, if not wholly unexplored, had not, however, been surveyed before with equal minuteness of observation.

[* Some of the vessels indeed were larger. "Il y avoit vingt-deux hommes dans la plus grande, dans les moyennes, huit ont dix, deux ou trois dans les plus petites. Ces pirogues paroissoient bien faites; elles ont l'avant et l'amere fort relévés, etc. Ils portent des bracelets, et des plaques au front et sur le col. J'ignore de quelle matiere, elle m'a paru etre blanche." Boug. Chap. v. p. 264.]

Lieutenant Shortland now congratulated himself on having cleared this large tract of land, which he had the greatest reason to suppose united the whole way from the place at which he first fell in with it; as in sailing at a very moderate distance from the coast, he had made every effort in his power to find a passage to the northward. A place called by one of the French navigators, Port Surville, is probably a part of it, as well as Choiseul Bay, but the points seen and described by the French discoverers are very few; and for the knowledge of the form and bearings of the rest of the coast, throughout the whole extent of near three degrees of latitude, and full five of longitude, we are indebted entirely to the researches of our own countryman, as we are for the beautiful delineation of the whole coast, to the care and ingenuity of his son, Mr. John George Shortland. The only places in which Lieutenant Shortland suspected there might possibly be a passage which had escaped his observation, was between Cape Phillip and Cape Henslow, and again between the capes Marsh and Pitt. The ascertaining of these matters he leaves to other navigators, at the same time recommending the route he took as the safest and most expeditious passage within his knowledge from Port Jackson to China; Middleton Shoal, on the coast of New South Wales, being the only place of danger he had hitherto discovered. Should any objection be made to passing through a strait, where a more open sea can be obtained, he would recommend the much wider channel between Egmont Island and Simboo, and not by any means the whole circuit to the east of the New Hebrides. To the whole of this land, consisting of the two principal islands on each side of the straits, and the Treasury Isles between them, Lieutenant Shortland gave the name of New Georgia. There is, indeed, an island of Georgia, to the east of Staten Land, so named by Captain Cook in 1775: but between these, it seems to be a sufficient distinction to call the one the Isle of Georgia, and the other New Georgia. The land on the western side of Shortland's Straits, continued to be very high, and extended as far as the eye could reach; from these circumstances, and from the direction in which it trended, no doubt was entertained of its joining that which was called by Captain Carteret, Lord Anson's Isle. With respect to the charts here given of these discoveries, Lieutenant Shortland, though he cannot, from the distance at which they were taken, presume to vouch for the laying down of every single point, as if the coast had undergone a regular survey, undertakes to promise, that they are sufficiently accurate for the direction of any future navigators; as he had, in the course of his progress along it, many opportunities of taking lunar observations.

Shortland's Chart of New Georgia

9 August 1788

At six in the afternoon of Saturday, August 9th, the extreme point in sight of the high land to the westward of the passage, bore south-west by south, distant twelve or fourteen leagues: and two islands which the ship had just made, bore north-west by north, distant five or six leagues. They are supposed to lie in latitude 4° 50' south, and longitude 156° 11' east. At day light on Sunday August 10th, Lieutenant Shortland set his steering sails, and bore away to the north-west, in order to make more distinctly the islands seen the preceding evening.

10 August 1788

At six in the morning, four were in sight, and bore south-west, distant six leagues. It was at first thought that they would prove to be the nine islands seen by Captain Carteret; but as neither the number nor the longitude was found to correspond, Lieutenant Shortland afterwards concluded they were not the same; and determined, as the weather appeared squally and unsettled, not to attempt pursuing the tract of that officer through St. George's Channel, but to go round New Ireland.

Chapter XIX.

August 1788 to February 1789

Appearance of the scurvy--The boats land at one of the Pelew Islands--Account of the Natives who were seen, and conjectures concerning them--Distresses--The *Friendship* cleared and sunk--Miserable condition of the *Alexander* when she reached Batavia.--Conclusion.

10 August 1788

Hitherto no difficulties had been encountered but such as necessarily attend the exploring of new coasts, wherein the anxiety is fully compensated by the satisfaction of becoming a discoverer: but a dreadful scourge now hung over our navigators, the severity of which cannot easily be conceived, even by those who have been placed in similar scenes, so much did it exceed in degree every thing of the same kind that has been usually experienced. It was about this time, the 10th of August, that the scurvy began to make its appearance, which, for want of the proper remedies, increased to a malignity that was destructive of many lives, rendered it necessary to sacrifice one of the ships, and finally reduced the consolidated crews of both in the remaining transport to such a state of weakness, that without immediate assistance they must have perished even in port, or would have been driven adrift again, from total inability to take the necessary steps for their own preservation.

13 August 1788

On the thirteenth of August, five seamen of the *Alexander* were already on the sick list, complaining of pains in the legs and breast, with their gums so swelled, and their teeth so loose that they could not without difficulty eat even flour or rice. The weather was now very variable, often sultry, at other times squally, with occasional showers. The ships were probably at no great distance from some land, as birds were frequently seen in great numbers; and on the 16th the *Friendship* made the signal for seeing land, but it could not be descried from the *Alexander.* Sharks were also caught with the hook, and now and then some floating wood and vegetables were observed. On this day the two transports passed the equator. On the 24th, Lieutenant Shortland found by observation, that a current had set the ship to the west north-west or north-west by west of her account, at the rate of eleven miles a day since the 13th, when the last lunar observation had been taken.

The scurvy gained ground rapidly in the *Alexander*, notwithstanding the precautions of smoking the ship, washing with vinegar, and distributing porter, spruce-beer, and wine among the seamen. On the 2d of September six men and a boy, on the 5th eight, and on the 8th ten, were disabled by it from performing any duty. An increase of this kind, in the midst of all the efforts that could be made to counteract the malignity of the disorder, gave but too certain a prognostic of the ravages it was afterwards to make.

10 September 1788

About noon on the 10th of September, the looming of land was discerned to the westward, which an hour after was clearly perceived, bearing west north-west, at the distance of six leagues. As the ships were then in latitude about 6° 49' north, and longitude 135° 25' east, it is evident that this must have been one of the Pelew Islands, lately so much celebrated for their hospitable reception of Captain Wilson and his crew. As the account of that voyage was not then published, and Lieutenant Shortland had no charts with him that noticed these islands, he concluded that he was among the most southern of the New Carolines; but finding his longitude, from accurate observation, to be more westerly than the situation of those islands, he conceived their longitude to be laid down in the charts erroneously.

11 September 1788

At six in the morning, September 11th, a small island not seen before, bore west south-west, distant five leagues; and the wind coming round to the south south-west, Lieutenant Shortland bore away for the passage between the two islands. At nine, having entered the passage, he founded and found thirteen fathoms, with a fine sandy bottom, and a strong current setting through very rapidly. Many cocoa-palms were seen on the shore, and excited an earnest expectation of procuring effectual refreshment for the sick: a boat from each of the ships was therefore manned and sent out. While the boats were sounding a-head, many Indians approached in their canoes, and by signs invited our people to shore, giving them to understand that they might be supplied with cocoa nuts and many other things; but when they attempted to land at a place which had the appearance of a Morai or burying-place, they would not suffer it, insisting that they should proceed further one way or the other. In the mean time many persons of both sexes swam off from shore, holding up bamboos* full of water, which they imagined the ships to want. Mr. Sinclair, the Master of the *Alexander*, being in the boat, brought the following account of this expedition. "Finding I could not make them understand that I wanted cocoa-nuts, and not water, I was resolved to land, and therefore put on shore as soon as I found a convenient place, amidst a concourse of between three and four hundred people. I immediately fixed upon an old man, (whom, from an ornament of bone upon his arm, I concluded to be a chief) and made him a present of some nails and beads, which were accepted with evident pleasure, and immediately conciliated his friendship. This was a fortunate step, as he afterwards often showed his authority by checking the most insolent of his people when they pressed forward and endeavoured to steal whatever they could seize. One seaman holding his cutlass rather carelessly had it snatched from him, and the thief had so well watched his opportunity, that he was almost out of sight before he was distinguished. Notwithstanding the offers of the natives in the canoes, I could not procure above thirty cocoanuts, and those green; whether it was that the people did not comprehend my signs, or that they were not inclined to carry on the traffic. These islanders were well limbed men, moderately tall, with long hair: many of them chewed the betel nut, and these were all furnished with a small hollow stick, apparently of ebony, out of which they struck a kind of powder like lime* Their arms were a lance, and a kind of adze hung over the shoulder; some men carrying one, and others two. These adzes were of iron, and evidently of European manufacture. As the place where we landed was very rocky and unpleasant for walking, when I found myself unsuccessful in the chief object for which I was sent out, I returned as expeditiously as I could. In return for my presents, the old chief gave one to me which was not equally acceptable. It was a mixture of fish, yams, and many other things, the odour of which, probably from the staleness of the composition, was very far from being agreeable. When we first landed, many of the natives repeated the word, Englees, as if to enquire whether we were of that nation, but when they understood that we were they shook their heads and said, Espagnol: possibly, therefore, the discovery of our nation might prevent them from being as courteous on shore as they had been in their canoes."

[* Bamboos were the only water vessels in the Pelew Islands. See Wilson, chap. xxv. p. 312.]

[* This was the Chinam, or coral, burnt to lime, always used with the betel. See Wilson's Account, p. 27. The Areca is the nut, the leaves only of betel are used. These are produced by different plants.]

From some of the above circumstances it is undeniably evident that these people have had intercourse with Europeans, and probably with the Spaniards; and from the aversion which they expressed to the English, it seems not an unfair conjecture that this island might perhaps be Artingall, where our countrymen had distinguished themselves five years before by the assistance they gave to a hostile state*: but if so, their knowledge of the Spaniards must have been posterior to the departure of the English, who from the narrative must have been the first Europeans seen there. Had the adventures of the Antelope's crew been then made known to the world, Lieutenant Shortland would with joy have presented himself before the beneficent Abba Thulle; and probably by obtaining a stock of fresh provisions and vegetables might have preserved the lives of many of his companions, and prevented the sufferings of the rest; but he was not fortunate enough to know that so propitious a retreat was within so small a distance.

[* It might, perhaps, be thought by some readers, that if this had been the case they would now have endeavoured to take revenge, but we find from Captain Wilson's narrative, that all animosity was dropped as soon as peace had been established with the inhabitants of Pelew. See that work, Chap. xvi. p. 192.]

23 September 1788

His people were doomed to find their distresses augmented instead of diminished. Towards the latter end of September, agues and intermittent fevers began to prevail among them; the proportion of those disabled by the scurvy was constantly great, some deaths had happened, and the few men who still had health enough to carry them with difficulty through the necessary duty, were subject to the swelling of the legs, and harrassed by violent pains in the breast. Hitherto the *Friendship* had been much more happily circumstanced. On the 23d of September she was spoken to, and had then only one man disabled by the scurvy: but this advantage was of short duration, and the more rapid increase of the malady made a fatal compensation for the greater delay of its commencement.

27 September 1788-19 October 1788

On the 27th of September, about noon, the *Alexander* made the land of Mindanao. It bore from west by north to north-west by west, distant fourteen leagues. Part of it was remarkably high, and at this distance appeared like a separate island, but on a nearer approach was found to be all connected. On the 30th, about four in the afternoon, Hummock Island bore west by south, half south, distant six or seven leagues. In all this sea a strong current constantly set the ship considerably to the south of her reckoning. On the third of October the wind fell suddenly, and the *Alexander* being in great danger of driving with the current upon the shore of Karkalang or Sanguir Island, was obliged to drop her anchor, which happily brought her up in forty fathoms water. In the evening of the 17th, the *Friendship* actually struck upon a reef on the coast of Borneo, when the *Alexander* immediately cast anchor, and sent a boat to her assistance; but at day light the next morning it appeared that she also lay so encompassed with sand-keys and shoals, that it was difficult to discern how she had sailed into that situation, or what track she must pursue to be extricated from it. The *Friendship*, however, fortunately got off from the reef without sustaining any material damage: and in the morning of the nineteenth a narrow channel was found, through which the *Alexander* with difficulty sailed out of her dangerous station. Attempts had been made to weigh anchor the preceding day, but the wind failing, the force of the currents prevented it. The ships were at this time not more than eight leagues from the coast of Borneo.

The scurvy had now brought both the crews to a most pitiable situation. The *Alexander* had lost eight of her complement, and was reduced to two men in a watch, only four seamen and two boys being at all fit for duty: and though these were willing to do their best, and further encouraged by the promise of double wages when they should arrive at Batavia, their utmost exertions were inadequate to the necessities of the ship, which they were hardly able to put about; nor could they have weighed even a small anchor had the currents obliged them to bring to again. The *Friendship* had only five men not disabled, and was by no means well provided with provisions. In this melancholy state of both ships, the western monsoon being expected soon to set in, it was indispensably necessary to give up one for the sake of preserving the other. Upon this subject the masters consulted, and after some time came to an agreement. As the *Friendship* was the smaller vessel, and would be cleared more easily than the *Alexander*, having fewer stores on board, Mr. Walton, her master, consented that she should be evacuated and sunk, on condition that he should be allowed half freight of the *Alexander*. In four days the *Friendship* had her crew and stores transferred to the *Alexander*, after which she was bored and turned adrift. The ships company thus made out from both vessels was of no great strength, not amounting to half the proper complement of the *Alexander*, nor was it more than, allowing for the further ravages of disease, was absolutely necessary to work that ship to Batavia.

The following list contains the whole number of persons now on board the *Alexander*. BELONGING TO THE *Alexander*. In Health. Lieutenant Shortland, Commander. Duncan Sinclair, Master. W. A. Long, first Mate. T. G. Shortland, second ditto. John Winter, Seamen. Ant. Hedley, Edward Waters, John Lewis, Thomas Frazer, Boys. John White Sick. Charles Clay, Seamen. James Stockell, Robert Ranson, William Dixon, Boy. FROM THE FRIENDSHIP. Well. Francis Walton, Master. Robert Laurence, first Mate. J. Walton, second Mate. Robert Barnes, Boatswain. William Hern, Steward. William Bruce, Cook. James Craven, Seamen. William Allen Sick. John Philpot, Corp. Corn. Du Heg, Seamen. R. Smith, Robert George, Rich. Sandell, John Morris, Robert Cockran, Lieutenant Collins, a passenger.

29 October 1788

On the 29th of October, at five in the morning, a land wind springing up from the coast of Borneo, within six miles of which the *Alexander* had lain at anchor, she got again under way, and at ten was abreast of the point that forms the entrance into the harbour of Pamanookan. At five in the afternoon Pulo Laoot bore from south-south-west to south-west by south, distant twelve or fourteen leagues; but the wind being now southerly, and the current strongly against the vessel, she did not get round this island till November the 5th.

1 November 1788

Wine was constantly served in due proportions to the sick and well, but neither that, nor any other remedy that could be tried amended the condition of the people. Sickness continued to spread among them, insomuch that in the beginning of November only one man besides the officers was able to go aloft. A short alarm by no means added to the comfort of their condition: on the first of this month four large boats, three of which rowed eighteen oars, and the fourth not less than twelve or fourteen, bore down upon the ship, apparently with hostile intentions. When they approached within about a mile they lay to, as if to consult with each other, and then continued to row and sail after the *Alexander.* Lieutenant Shortland hoisted English colours, which one of the boats answered by hoisting Dutch, and another Portugueze colours. They continued in chase till five in the afternoon, and it was imagined that their design was to board and seize the ship in the night. During the pursuit the little strength that could be raised was put in motion, all were stationed at their quarters, and the carronades and great guns put in order. When these preparations were made, Lieutenant Shortland determined to show his own resolution, and to try that of his assailants, by firing a shot in a direct line over them. This was done accordingly, and fully answered the intention, for they immediately desisted from the pursuit, and made hastily for the shore.

Had the *Alexander* been at this time a very few days sail more distant from Batavia, she must inevitably have been lost, not from any stress of weather, or danger of coasts or shoals, but merely from inability to conduct her into port, as every man on board must have been totally disabled.

17 November 1788

On the 17th of November only one man was fit for work, besides the officers; a very little longer continuance would have reduced her to the condition of floating at the mercy of winds and waves, without any possibility of assisting, impeding, or directing her course. At six that evening, the wind being too scanty to carry her into the roads of Batavia, an effort was made by all indiscriminately who were able to work, and anchor was cast between the islands of Leyden and Alkmara; soon after a gun was fired, and a signal made for assistance. At two in the afternoon on the 18th, as no assistance arrived, the still greater effort of weighing anchor was tried, and the task performed with the utmost difficulty; after which, standing in with the sea breeze, the ship came again to anchor at five, in nine fathoms. The boat was now hoisted out, and sent to beg assistance from the Dutch Commodore, the crew of the *Alexander* being so much reduced as to be unable to furl their own sails. A party was immediately sent to assist, and six of the Dutch seamen remained on board all night, lest any blowing weather should come on. Never, perhaps, did any ship arrive in port more helpless, without being shattered by weather, from the mere effects of a dreadful and invincible disorder.

19 November 1788-7 December 1788

At five in the morning of the 19th, the welcome sight appeared of a boat from the Dutch Commodore, which he had humanely laded with refreshments. She brought also a boatswain's mate and twelve seamen to assist in refitting the ship for sea. The sick were sent on the 20th to the hospital, where several of them died, being too far gone for any accommodation or skill to recover. From the Bridgewater and Contractor East Indiamen, which lay in the road when the *Alexander* arrived; and from the Raymond, Asia, and Duke of Montrose, which came in a few days after; with the assistance of a few men from the Dutch Commodore, a fresh crew was at length made up, in which only four of the original seamen remained, the rest being either dead, or not enough recovered to return with the *Alexander*, when she sailed again on the 7th of December.

18 February 1789

The remaining part of the voyage was attended with few circumstances worthy of notice, and was made in a track sufficiently known to all navigators to permit us to dispense with a minute description of it. At the Cape they met with Captain Hunter, in the *Sirius,* who, when the *Alexander* arrived, on the 18th of February, 1789, had been in Table Bay six weeks. From him Lieutenant Shortland learned that the *Borrowdale* and the *Prince of Wales* transports, which had parted from him on the coast of New South Wales, had returned by the southern passage, and had been heard of from Rio de Janeiro. In Table Bay the *Alexander* remained at anchor till the 16th of March, when she sailed again, and arrived off the Isle of Wight on the 28th of May.

Thus concluded a voyage, the first part of which was enlivened and rendered important by discoveries; the next involved in gloom through the virulent attacks of distemper, and the frequent inroads of death. Much was certainly performed, and very much was suffered, but from the whole we are authorized to conclude, that the settlement of our countrymen on the new southern continent, must powerfully tend to the improvement of navigation, and the extension of geographical knowledge. Nor is it necessary, that any ill-omened apprehensions should be excited by the misfortunes of the *Alexander* and the *Friendship*. It may not happen again that ships shall quit Port Jackson so ill prepared with antidotes against the malignant poison of the scurvy: nor, if they should, is it by any means certain that their visitation will be equally severe.

Chapter XX.

Lieutenant Watts's Narrative of the Return of the *Lady Penrhyn*Transport; containing an Account of the Death of Omai, and other interesting Particulars at Otaheite.

5 May 1788-17 May 1788

The *Lady Penrhyn*, Capt. Sever, left Port Jackson on the 5th of May, 1788. In the evening of the 7th, imagining they saw a fire on shore, they sounded, but found no bottom with ninety fathoms of line. By their observation at noon, on the 9th, they found a current had set the vessel eighty miles to the southward since their leaving Port Jackson. The scurvy began already to make its appearance amongst them; one man was rendered unfit for duty, and several others complained very much. The weather in general was squally, with thunder, lightning, and rain. In the morning of the 14th they saw an island bearing north-east, half north, 18 or 20 leagues distant, which made in two detached hummocks: At seven in the afternoon, the island seen in the morning was about nine leagues distant, on which they brought to for the night, and next morning made sail and stood for it. At noon they spoke to the *Supply*, Lieutenant Ball, who informed them that this island is named Lord Howe's Island. During the afternoon and night they stood off and on, and at nine o'clock the next morning a boat was hoisted out, and Lieutenant Watts with a party went on shore in search of turtle, but they could distinguish no traces of any, though the different bays were very closely explored: about noon, Mr. Watts returned on board. This disappointment did not deter them from making another effort, as some turtle would have been a very valuable acquisition: accordingly Mr. Anstis went with a party in the pinnace to try his success in the night. About noon the next day Mr. Anstis returned without having seen one turtle, but to make some amends, the party had met with great success in fishing, having caught a sufficient quantity to serve the ship's company three or four days.

Lord Howe's Island was discovered by Lieutenant Ball on his passage to Norfolk Island in the month of February, and on his return he stopt and surveyed it; at that time he caught a quantity of fine green turtles, of which there were great numbers: this induced Governor Phillip to send the *Supply*a second time to this island, but she then was unsuccessful, the weather probably being so cold as to occasion the turtle to remove to the northward. The island is about two leagues in extent, and lies in the direction of north 30° west, and south 30° east; the south-east end making in two very high mounts, which may be seen at the distance of more than twenty leagues, and at first appear like two detached isles. About three leagues from these, and nearly in a south-east direction, is a remarkably high and pointed rock,* which may be seen at least twelve leagues off; from this there are dangerous rocks extending three or four miles, both in a south-east and south-west line; those to the south-west not shewing themselves above water: there are also rocks extending four or five miles off the north-west and north-east ends of the island, which is of a moderate height. Both extremes are bluff, and there appears to be much foul ground about them: within the north-west point lies a rock with eleven fathoms water close to it, and there is a passage between it and the island. The reef on the west side extends nearly to both extremes with breaks in it, through which boats may pass with safety, but within the reef it is in general very shoaly. The island is tolerably broad at each end, and very narrow, with low land in the center, forming two bays, that should the wind be from south-east to north-east, or south-west to north-west, a ship may always be secure by running to the leeward of the island. There are regular soundings on the west side, but the ground is too hard for holding well, being coral rocks. The east side they did not examine. The low narrow part has evidently been overflowed and the island disjointed, for in the very center, as they walked across, they saw large beds of coral rocks, and shells in great abundance; and on the east side, which seems in general to be the weather side, the sea has thrown up a bank of sand, from twenty-five to thirty feet in height, which serves as a barrier against future inundations. The island has likewise every appearance of having undergone a volcanic revolution, as they found great quantities of burnt stone and pumice stone; and Mr. Anstis, who landed on the reef which shelters the west bay, at dead low water, found the whole a burnt up mass.

[* Ball's Pyramid.]

The inhabitants of this island were all of the feathered tribe, and the chief of these was the ganet, of which there were prodigious numbers, and it should seem that this is the time of their incubation, the females being all on their nests: these are places simply hollowed in the sand, there not being a single quadruped that could be found upon the island to disturb them. The people brought numbers of their eggs on board. Very large pigeons were also met with in great plenty; likewise beautiful parrots and parroquets; a new species, apparently, of the coote, and also of the rail, and magpie; and a most beautiful small bird, brown, with a yellow breast and yellow on the wing; it seemed to be a species of humming bird: there was also a black bird, like a sheerwater, with a hooked bill, which burrows in the ground. Numbers of ants were seen, which appeared the only insect at this place, except the common earth worm. The soil is of a sandy nature, and fresh water extremely scarce in those places which they had an opportunity of examining.

This island is well covered with wood, the chief of which is the large and dwarf mangrove, the bamboo, and the cabbage tree. The different vegetables met with were scurvy grass, wild celery, spinach, endive, and samphire.

31 May 1788

From the mean of all their observations they found this island to be situated in 31°. 30'. 49". south latitude, and by comparing their lunar observations with those of Lieutenant Ball, they found its longitude to be 159°. 10'. 00". east of Greenwich. The mean state of the thermometer, during their short stay, was 66°. and the variation of the compass, by many observations, was found to be 10°. east. In the afternoon the pinnace was hoisted in, and they made sail to the eastward with a fresh breeze at south-west. Nothing material occurred till the 31st, when about three o'clock in the afternoon they saw two islands, one bearing north-east, half east, seven leagues, and the other east by south, about six leagues distant. Not having an opportunity of getting well in with the land before night came on, they plied occasionally under an easy sail, and at day-light next morning [1 June 1788] made sail and bore up for it. On approaching the southernmost land, they found it to form two barren isles, separated by a channel about a quarter of a mile over, and apparently free from danger: the north island lies in a north half east direction from these, and about five leagues distant. At noon, the body of the north island bore north-east by north three miles distant: their latitude at that time was 30°. 11'. south, and the longitude by lunar observation 180°. 58'. 37". east. At one o'clock they bore round the west end of the island, and hove to near the center of it, about a mile off shore. They were in hopes, from the appearance of the island at a distance, that they should have found it productive of something beneficial to the people, (the scurvy gaining ground daily) but they were greatly disappointed; both the north and south sides are surrounded by rocks, over which the water flows, without the least opening for a boat; however, Capt. Sever ordered the small boat to be hoisted out, and went on shore accompanied by Mr. Anstis: they found great difficulty in landing, and, when upon the rocks, they had to mount a very dangerous precipice, in order to gain the level part of the island. This island forms very high at the west end, and slopes gradually to the east end, where it terminates in a cliff of a moderate height: both sides have a range of these cliffs extending the whole length, which are chiefly composed of white sand. The whole of the island bears the strongest marks of being a volcanic production, having great quantities of pumice stone on it, and the rocks quite burnt up. The top of the land was covered with a coarse kind of grass, and the place affords great plenty of the wild mangrove. The extent of this island is about two miles and an half, nearly in the direction of east-south-east and west-north-west; the soil a mixture of mould and sand. The inhabitants are the brown gull, the light-grey bird, ganets, and a parroquet of the same species with those met with at Lord Howe's Island. The gentlemen could scarcely walk a step without being up to the knee in holes: they saw a great number of rats and mice, and found many birds lying dead at the entrances of their burrows: they saw no appearance of fresh water, though from the gullies that were formed in various parts, the island must certainly be subject to very heavy rains. This island was named Macaulay's Island, after G. M. Macaulay, Esq; and the two islands to the southward, Curtis's Isles, after Timothy and William Curtis, Esqrs. At five in the afternoon, the Captain returning on board, the boat was hoisted in, and they made sail, standing to the eastward with a moderate breeze at south-west. Macaulay's Island is situated in 30°. 09'. south latitude, and 180°. 58'. 37". east longitude.

Curtis's Isles

Macaulay's Isles

6 June 1788-10 July 1788

The scurvy now began to spread very fast among the crew, and by the 6th, they had nine men unable to get out of their hammocks, and many others complained very much: swelled gums, the flesh exceeding black and hard, a contraction of the sinews, with a total debility; were the general appearances. Wine was daily served out to them, and there was sour-krout on on board, but the people refused to eat it. From this to the 17th they had little variety; by that time the people were in a deplorable state, for with every person on board, the Captain included, they could only muster ten men able to do duty, and some of them were in a very weakly state: sour-krout, which before had been refused, now began to be sought after, and they had all the Captain's fresh stock, himself and officers living solely on salt provisions; and to add to their melancholy situation the wind hung almost constantly in the eastern board, so that they could scarcely make any progress. For several days they had very squally unsettled weather, attended with almost constant heavy rain, and frequent storms of thunder and lightning. On the 24th, being then in 32°. 12'. south latitude, and 207°. 28'. east longitude, the wind shifted to the westward, but the weather still continued squally and unsettled. On the 7th July, in 21°. 57'. south latitude, they fell in with the south-east trade wind, and as the people were in a very weak condition, it was determined to make Otaheite as soon as possible. At six o'clock in the morning of the 9th, they saw Osnaburgh Island, bearing north by east, half east, four or five leagues distant. At seven they bore up for Otaheite, and at ten o'clock that island made its appearance, bearing west by north; by five in the afternoon they were abreast of Oaitepeha Bay, and ten canoes presently came alongside with bread-fruit, cocoa nuts, etc. The Indians pressed them very much to come to an anchor there, but as they were not able to purchase their anchor again when once let go, Mr. Watts advised the Captain to stand on for Matavai Bay. During the night they wore occasionally, and at day-light in the morning of the 10th stood in for the land. At noon, Point Venus bore south-west by south about three miles distant. In standing into Matavai Bay the ship got rather too close on the Dolphin Bank, having only two and a half fathoms water for several casts, over a hard bottom, but she deepened at once to seventeen fathoms, and they stood over to the south side of the bay, in hopes by making a board, to fetch the Resolution's old birth, which would have made the watering place very handy; but the ship missing stays, they were obliged to let go the anchor, and content themselves in their situation. They anchored at nine o'clock in eight fathoms water, over a soft bottom, Point Venus bearing north-north-east, and One Tree Hill south by east, half east, distant from shore about half a mile. On approaching the bay, they could perceive a prodigious number of the natives on Point Venus, and round the beach, and several canoes put off from the shore, the Indians waving pieces of white cloth and making signs for them to come into the bay. When anchored they had only three men in one watch, and two in the other besides the mates, and two of these ailing; the rest of the crew were in a truly deplorable state.

Their first care was naturally to procure some refreshments, and it was a pleasing circumstance for them to see the natives flock round the ship, calling out "Tayo Tayo," which signifies friends; and "Pahii no Tutti," Cook's ship; and bringing in very great plenty cocoa nuts, bread-fruit, plantains and taro, and a fruit known by the name of the Otaheite apple; they also brought some hogs and fowls. All the Indians appeared glad to see them, and disposed of their various commodities on very moderate terms, and indeed their whole behaviour indicated the most friendly intentions. In the evening, the Chief of Matavai came on board, and in him Lieutenant Watts recollected an old friend: the Chief was greatly pleased to see Mr. Watts, as he was the only person in the ship who had been here before, except the steward, who had been before the mast in the Resolution; therefore, when Mona (which was the chief's name) saw his old acquaintance, he explained to his companions who he was, and that he had been with Capt. Cook, and they seemed very glad to have some of their old visitors again. Mr. Watts learnt from Mona, that O'too was still living, that he was always called Earee Tutti, and then was absent on a visit to the eastward, but expected to return in four or five days: At the same time, he said, messengers had been sent to acquaint him of the ship's arrival. He also informed Mr. Watts, that Maheine, the chief of Eimeo, to retaliate the mischief done him by Capt. Cook, had, after the departure of the Resolution and Discovery from the islands, landed in the night at Oparree, and destroyed all the animals and fowls he could lay hold of, and that O'too was obliged to fly to the mountains. He likewise intimated that the Attahooroo men joined Maheine in this business. Indeed, it occurred to Mr. Watts, that when here in the Resolution, Toha, the chief of that district, threatened something of the kind in a quarrel with O'too, and probably smothered his resentment only for a time, fearful of Capt. Cook revenging it, should it come to his knowledge.

11 July 1788

The next day, Oediddee agreeably surprised them with a visit on board: he was greatly rejoiced to see them, and enquired after all his friends in a very affectionate manner: He took great pleasure in recounting his route in the Resolution, had treasured up in his memory the names of the several places he had been at in her, nor had he forgot his English compliments. He informed them that no ship had been at the islands since Capt. Cook: therefore, they concealed his death, and Capt. Sever made Oediddee a present, as coming from Capt. Cook. Oediddee confirmed the report of the cattle, etc. being destroyed by Maheine, and likewise informed them that Omai, and the two New Zealand boys had been dead a considerable time through illness, and that one horse only was alive at Huaheine, but they could not learn any further particulars from him.

13 July 1788

In the evening of the 13th, a messenger came on board with a present from O'too of a small pig, a dog, and some white cloth, and intimated that he would be at Matavai the next day. Early in the next morning but few canoes came off to the ship, and the natives were observed assembling on the shore in prodigious numbers: soon afterwards, a canoe came alongside and informed them that O'too was on the beach; on this, the Captain and Mr. Watts went on shore immediately, and found him surrounded by an amazing concourse of people, amongst whom were several women cutting their foreheads very much with the shark's tooth, but what both surprised and pleased them very much, was, to see a man carrying the portrait of Captain Cook, drawn by Webber in 1777. Notwithstanding so much time had elapsed since the picture was drawn, it had received no injury, and they were informed that O'too always carried it with him wherever he went. After the first salutations were over, Mr. Watts asked O'too to accompany him to the ship, to which he readily agreed; but previously to his entering the boat he ordered the portrait in, and when he got alongside the ship he observed the same ceremony. When on board he appeared much pleased, asked after his old friends, and was very particular in his enquiries after Capt. Cook. He visited the ship between decks, was astonished to see so few people on board, and the greatest part of them in a debilitated state, and enquired if they had lost any men at sea. He acquainted them with the revenge taken by the Eimeo people, and asked why they had not brought out some cattle, etc. He also mentioned the death of Omai, and the New Zealand boys, and added, that there had been a skirmish between the men of Uliatea and those of Huaheine, in which the former were victorious, and that a great part of Omai's property was carried to Uliatea. O'too was considerably improved in his person, and was by much the best made man of any that they saw; nor was he, as yet, disfigured by the baneful effects of the ava. He preserved his original character in supplying the ship with provisions of every kind in the most liberal manner; and when any of the natives who had come from a considerable distance, begged his intercession with them on board to take their hogs, etc. off their hands, which, on account of the few people they had, they were often obliged, much against their inclination, to refuse, he was very moderate: indeed, he generally left the matter to themselves, and whenever he undertook to dispose of another person's property was always well paid for his trouble. During their stay at Otaheite he daily paid them a visit, and importuned the Captain very much to move the ship into the Resolution's old birth: where she then lay, she was nearly in the situation of the Dolphin on her first anchoring; and though at some distance from the watering place, yet, considering the small number of people on board, and their weak situation, the Captain judged it prudent to remain where he was, as in case of necessity he could put to sea instantly.

O'too was always accompanied by a woman, whose advice he asked upon every occasion; she was by no means handsome, neither did she possess that delicacy, or those engaging manners that so much distinguish her countrywomen in general: she was of the Earree class, and seemed to have great authority; but whether or no she was his wife they did not learn, though Mr. Watts was rather inclined to think they were married, and he appeared to be greatly attached to her. The king and all the chiefs were very urgent for Captain Sever to go to Eimeo, and revenge their quarrel, and several of them offered to get a stock of provisions and accompany him; however, to this request he gave a positive refusal. About three days before they quitted Matavai Bay, O'too brought the ring of an anchor on board, observing it might be made into small hatchets: Mr. Watts upon examining it, recollected that it certainly belonged to an anchor which Captain Cook bought of Opooni, at Bola Bola, in 1777: as there was no forge on board the *Lady Penrhyn*, the Captain offered O'too three hatchets for it, which he readily took. When Captain Cook bought the anchor just mentioned it wanted the ring and one of the palms, and at that time they knew that it had been carried from Otaheite, and belonged to Mons. Bougainville: how O'too came by the ring, Mr. Watts could not learn, but had he possessed it when the Resolution was here, it is reasonable to suppose he would have brought it to Captain Cook, and the more so as at that time the natives used to bring many large pieces of iron (which they had obtained from the Spaniards) to be either worked up or exchanged for trinkets. Though from the season of the year they had reason to expect a scarcity of vegetables, yet they were agreably surprised to find them in the greatest plenty and profusion; hogs were multiplied amazingly, and from the proceedings of the natives, Mr. Watts was induced to think they were desirous to thin them, as they brought none to barter but sows, and the greatest part of them were with pig: fowls were obtained in tolerable plenty, but they were all cocks, and old; the natives likewise brought goats alongside for sale, and some of them brought cats and offered them in barter. Captain Sever purchased a fine male and milch goat with two kids.

Cocoa nuts are a never failing article at this place, and the bread-fruit, which was so scarce when the Endeavour was here at the same season of the year, was now exceedingly plentiful, and in high perfection, as was the Otaheite apple; plantains, both ripe and green, and taro, the natives brought in great quantities, but yams and sweet potatoes were very scarce. They purchased seven or eight dozen of pumkins, and a quantity of chilipods, which were some of the produce of the Resolution's garden, and one of the Indians brought some cabbage leaves on board, but the cabbages, as well as sundry other vegetables, were gone to ruin for want of proper care and attention. The natives could not be enticed to eat any of the pumkins, and the chilipods they said poisoned them.

It already has been observed, that no ship of any nation had visited this island since Captain Cook, and from appearances, the iron which the natives obtained at that time was pretty well exhausted, as the only iron now seen was the blade of a table-knife; neither did they bring any tools on board to be sharpened, which certainly would have been the case had they been possessed of any, and such was their avidity to obtain hatchets, knives, etc. that every produce the island afforded was purchased at very reasonable rates, nor were the first prices given, attempted to be altered during their stay. Besides hatchets, knives, and nails, the natives were very desirous to have gimlets, files, and scissars; they also asked for looking-glasses, and white transparent beads, but of these latter articles they had none on board: red feathers, which had formerly been held in great esteem, were now of no value; they would accept them as presents indeed, but would not barter any one article for them.

As their situation was not a very eligible one, Mr. Watts did not think it prudent to go any great distance from the ship, or even to be much on shore, so that he was prevented from gaining much information, or seeing into many matters that might have enabled him to judge whether the whole of their report respecting Omai, and the loss of his property, etc. was true or not; however, he was inclined to think that the cattle and all the animals were killed, except goats, as Oediddee, when he confirmed the revenge of the Eimeo people, never mentioned that any one animal was saved: goats, indeed, had been left on former voyages, and from increase had become the property of many, but Maheine's resentment, it seems, was levelled at O'too only.

23 July 1788

Great numbers of the natives had been carried off by the venereal disease, which they had caught from their connections with the crews of the Resolution and Discovery; nor were the women so free from this complaint as formerly, especially the lowest class, the better sort seemingly not wishing to hazard the catching so terrible a disorder. The people having recovered in a most astonishing manner, and being now able to assist in the duties of the ship, Captain Sever thought it adviseable to run down amongst the Society Isles, as they had got a plentiful supply of provisions on board; accordingly, they got under way before daylight in the morning of the 23d. The natives soon took the alarm, and the breeze slackening, they were soon crowded with visitors, none of whom came empty handed. Their friends parted from them with great reluctance, and the suddenness of their departure seemed to disappoint the natives greatly; indeed, they would not have left the place so abruptly, had they not been apprehensive that if their intention was known, the Indians would have flocked on board in too great numbers, and have been troublesome. They had the satisfaction of leaving this Island in perfect amity with the natives, and it is but doing them justice to say, that during the time the *Lady Penrhyn* lay here, not one occasion offered to induce them to fire a musquet. Oediddee regretted their departure exceedingly, and importuned the Captain very much to take him to Uliatea, but O'too (whatever were his reasons) begged that he might by no means be taken from Otaheite; the Captain promised he should not, and taking leave of Oediddee, put him into his canoe, on which he shed tears in abundance, said he was very unhappy, and when he put from the ship never once turned to look at her: his situation was much to be pitied, and he truly merited every friendship that could be shown him; during the time they lay here, he was a constant visitor, and daily brought on board a supply of ready drest provisions. O'too was one of the earliest on board in the morning, and did not leave the ship till they had cleared the reef; he expressed great sorrow at their departure, mentioned how much time had elapsed since the Resolution and Discovery were at Otaheite, begged they would not be so long absent any more, and desired very much to have some horses brought to him, more particularly than any other animal: just before he quitted the ship, he asked for a few guns to be fired, with which the Captain complied. A breeze now springing up, their friends took a last farewell, and they stood to the north-west for Huaheine; at noon, Point Venus was about five miles distant.

It may, perhaps, be lamented, that Lieutenant Watts (whose acquaintance with the Chiefs, and knowledge of their language, rendered him a proper person to make enquiries) should not have been able to give a more full account of matters, at an island that has so much engaged the public notice; but, when the short stay of the ship, and her situation are considered, it will be natural to imagine, that the officers found their time very fully employed: such particulars, however, as have been above related may be depended on as facts.

25 July 1788

At noon on the 25th, they saw the island, Huaheine, bearing west three-quarters north, fourteen leagues distant: from this time they had very light winds, and those westerly, which prevented their reaching the island before noon on the 26th; when the extremes of it bore from west half north to south by west half west, off shore three miles. They kept standing off and on, on the east side (the wind continuing in the western board) till the 29th, during which time the natives brought off plenty of refreshments, but they were far more exorbitant in their demands than their neighbours.

29 July 1788

In the morning of the 29th, the wind veering to the south south-east, they stood round the north end of the island, and brought to off Owharree harbour; the natives appeared perfectly friendly, and constantly supplied them with every article except bread-fruit, which they said had failed that season: they were very importunate for them to go into the harbour, but as Captain Sever did not intend to stay more than a day or two, he did not think it worth the trouble.

In the evening, an elderly chief, who went by the name of Tutti, and whom Mr. Watts recollected to have frequently seen with Captain Cook, came on board; he confirmed the reports they had heard at Otaheite, and told them, that after Omai had got perfectly settled, he found himself under the necessity of purchasing a great quantity of cloth, and other necessaries, for himself and family, of which his neighbours took advantage, and made him pay extravagantly for every article he purchased; that he frequently visited Uliatea, and never went empty handed, so that by these means he expended much of his treasure: he died at his own house, as did the New Zealand boys, but in what order their deaths had happened, Tutti could not give information. Upon Omai's decease, the Uliatea men came over and attacked them for his property, alledging that as he was a native of their island they had an undoubted right to it. Tutti said they carried away a considerable part of his remaining property, and particularly his musquets, the stocks of which they broke, and took the powder and buried it in the sand: he added, that the conflict had been very fierce, and that great numbers were slain on both sides, nor were they friends even at this time. Three of the natives who came on board, had the os frontis fractured in a terrible manner, but they were then perfectly recovered of their wounds. The house that Captain Cook had built for Omai was still in being, and was covered by a very large one built after the country fashion; it was taken possession of by the chief of the island. With respect to the horses, the mare had foaled, but died soon afterwards, as did the foal, the horse was still living though of no benefit: thus were rendered fruitless the benevolent intentions of his Majesty, and all the pains and trouble Captain Cook had been at in preserving the cattle, during a tedious passage to these islands.

2 August 1788-24 August 1788

Having recruited their stock of provisions, and added a large quantity of yams and sugar cane, and the wind coming to the eastward (which had not been the case more than four or five days since their first anchoring in Matavai Bay) they on the 2d of August took leave of their friends, and stood to the northward until noon, when they steered north-west. They carried away from these hospitable islands, sixty hogs, weighing from seventy to two hundred and twenty pounds each, besides near fifty small pigs, ten dozen of fowls, an immense quantity of cocoa-nuts, green plantains, sugar cane, taro, and yams, and about eight dozen of pumkins; the people were all perfectly recovered, and from the plentiful stock of provisions on board there was reason to hope that they would not be any more alarmed for their safety. At day light in the Morning of the 8th, they saw a low flat island, bearing from east to north-east seven or eight miles distant; it appeared to be well clothed with trees, but the weather at that time being squally allowed them a very imperfect view. Captain Sever named it Penrhyn's Island; it is situated in 9°. 10'. south latitude, and 202°. 15'. east longitude. In the afternoon of the 20th, the Captain and some others imagining they saw land, and the sun setting in a fog-bank, which prevented them ascertaining the reality, they shortened sail, and lay by for the night; but at five o'clock the next morning no land being in sight, they made sail and stood to the north-west by west, with a fine breeze at north-east. In the evening of the 23d, being near the situation of an island and reef, as laid down in Lord Anson's chart, they brought to for the night. A number of ganets and other birds were flying about the next day, but no land appeared in sight: their latitude at noon was 9° 30' north, and 179° 18' east longitude.

15 September 1788

Nothing occured worthy of note till the 15th of September, when about noon they saw the island of Saypan, bearing west half north, twelve leagues distant. The next day at noon the south end of Tinian was about four leagues distant: in the afternoon the small boat was hoisted out, and Mr. Anstis went in her to sound a small bay round the south point of Saypan; he returned at seven o'clock, having found from ten to twenty fathoms water about a mile off shore, but the ground hard. The next morning, Mr. Anstis went on shore in the small boat to endeavour to procure a bullock, great numbers of which were seen grazing on the island Tinian. At six in the afternoon, they stood round the south point of Tinian, but finding they could not fetch into the road, they brought to for the night. In the evening, Mr. Anstis returned with the best part of a young bullock. The next morning at day light, they made sail and stood in for the road, and at nine o'clock came to anchor in eighteen fathoms, over a bottom of coral, about a mile and an half distant from shore. Soon after they anchored, a party were sent on shore to hunt.

25 September 1788-29 September 1788

From this to the 25th, they had light winds varying from south to east, with frequent showers over the land, and the flies so very troublesome that they found Captain Byron's account of them perfectly just. On coming to an anchor, they observed a buoy a little to the southward, with a slip buoy to it, they swept for the anchor, weighed it, and found it belonged to the*Charlotte* (Gilbert, master) one of the ships from Port Jackson bound to China; there were two-thirds of a cable to it. The party on shore also found some spars, apparently erected for a tent, and three water casks, one of which was full: it is most likely the *Charlotte* was blown out of the road, and could not regain her station again. Observing that their anchor was foul, on the 25th they hove it up to clear, and let it go again; presently afterwards, finding the ship adrift, they sounded, and had twenty-five fathoms, but as she was at the edge of the bank, they hove the anchor up, and made a stretch to the southward, but did not again fetch the bay till the evening of the 26th. The two following days they had dark heavy weather with very hard squalls, and almost continual rain, the wind from north-east to south-east. At day light in the morning of the 29th, the wind veered round to the south south-west, and soon afterwards, a very severe squall, attended with heavy rain, set the ship adrift, and the tide making strong to the north-west with a large hollow sea, they veered the reef very fast; however, the squall something abating, and fortunately backing round to the south south-east, they got their anchor up (which they otherwise would not have been able to have effected) and bore away to the north north-west. At noon the body of Tinian bore east half south, about four leagues distant.

During their stay at Tinian, filling water took up the whole of their time, the well not affording more than three tons a day, sometimes only two tons: the water was rather brackish, but otherwise not ill tasted. They found the fowls and hogs very shy, and the cattle had quite deserted the south part of the island, owing, as was imagined, to the alarm the *Charlotte*'s people had occasioned among them.

They obtained two bulls, eight hogs, and about a dozen fowls; they also got bread fruit, but it was at some distance up the country, and the generality of it not ripe: there was abundance of guavas but they were not in season; limes and sour oranges were also very plentiful. Cocoa-nut trees were in abundance, but those within a moderate distance from the beach were cut down, so that the distance they had to go for any was attended with too much fatigue to compensate for the advantages which could be derived from them, as they experienced from two or three attempts of the kind: the season in general seemed very backward. In addition to the animals of this place, they found wild cats, The country had exactly the same appearance as when Captains Byron and Wallis visited it, but many of the pyramidical pillars had fallen down and were much decayed. The mean state of the thermometer during their stay, was 87°. In their passage from hence to China, no material circumstance occurred, and on the 19th of October they anchored in Macao Roads.

Track of the *Scarborough*
Chapter XXI.

May 1788 to September 1788

The *Scarborough* leaves Port Jackson--Touches at Lord Howe's Island--Joins the *Charlotte*--Falls in with a large Shoal--Discover a number of Islands--Short account of the Inhabitants--Canoes described--Ornaments-- Discover Lord Mulgrave's Islands--Arrival at Tinian--Sick people sent on shore--Departure from Tinian--Arrival in Mocao Roads.

6 May 1788-22 May 1788

The *Scarborough* transport, Captain Marshall, left Port Jackson on the 6th of May 1788, and proceeded towards China, being engaged to take in a cargo of teas at Canton for the East India Company. For several days they had very unsettled weather, with frequent squalls and heavy rain. In the afternoon of the 16th, they saw Lord Howe's Island, bearing east by south seven leagues distant; and the next day at noon, they found the *Supply* brig, the *Lady Penrhyn*, and the *Charlotte*, standing off and on under the island. By two o'clock the *Scarborough* was close in with the land, but the weather not permitting them to go on shore, the night was spent in standing off and on.

Early the next morning, Captain Marshall sent his boat with the chief mate and six men on shore at Lord Howe's Island, in expectation of procuring some turtle, as the *Supply*, Lieutenant Ball, had caught a large quantity at this island in February: however, they were not able, after the most diligent search, to meet with any turtle; but this excursion was not altogether a fruitless one, for they brought off a quantity of fine birds, sufficient to serve the ship's crew three days; many of them were very fat, somewhat resembling a Guinea hen, and proved excellent food. Having procured such refreshments as the island afforded, they made sail at four o'clock, with the *Charlotte* in company, and stood to the eastward, with a moderate breeze at south-west. At eight o'clock in the morning of the 22d, they saw Norfolk Island, bearing east by south twelve leagues distant. At two o'clock, they were within one mile of the land, and had soundings in sixteen fathoms water over a hard bottom: the *Charlotte* being a considerable distance a-stern, Captain Marshall lay to for her to come up, and when she joined the *Scarborough* he stood under an easy sail to the distance of six leagues westward of the island, and carried soundings from sixteen to twenty-five fathoms, the ground various; in some places being soft, in other parts a corally bottom, and sometimes coarse white sand, intermixed with broken shells.

26 May 1788

After leaving Norfolk Island, they stretched to the northward and eastward, and at one o'clock on the twenty-sixth they saw a small island bearing north north-east eight or nine leagues distant; when about four miles from the island, they sounded with fifty fathoms of line, but got no bottom. Towards evening, Captain Marshall was close in with the island, and being desirous to examine it, he plied occasionally during the night. At day light the next morning, he was close to the land, and found it to be a barren rock, not more than half a mile over in the broadest part; it is very high, and was entirely covered with birds of various kinds, but there was no possibility of landing on account of a frightful surf that entirely surrounded it. This rock was seen first by Captain Gilbert, of the *Charlotte*, in the forenoon of the 26th, and named by him, Matthew's Island; it is situated in 22° 22' south latitude, and 170° 41' longitude, east of Greenwich.

30 May 1788-13 June 1788

On the 30th, in 17° 13' south latitude, and 172° 43' east longitude, they passed several large trees, and a number of cocoa-nuts floating in the water, but no land was to be seen. Nothing occurred worthy of note till the 4th of June, when the water appearing coloured, they sounded and struck the ground in fifteen fathoms water, although no land was to be seen: a man was then sent to the mast-head, who could plainly discern that the shoal run to the westward, on which Captain Marshall altered his course and stretched to the eastward, carrying soundings from fifteen to thirty fathoms water, over a rocky bottom, and in many places they could see the ground very distinctly. After running to the eastward, about eight miles, they found no bottom with seventy fathoms of line, which occasioned the Captain to tack and stand to the southward. Vast numbers of birds of different kinds were flying to the westward of the shoal, so that there probably is an island near that situation. The east part of this shoal is situated in 173° 12' east longitude, and the south part of it in 15° 50' south latitude, but how far it extends to the westward and northward is very uncertain, though doubtless to a considerable distance, as the water had a white appearance from the mast head as far as the eye could reach. Being now entirely free from the shoal, they stood to the northward, with a light easterly breeze, and moderate weather. On the 9th, in 7° 59' south latitude, the wind shifted to the westward and continued in the western board till the 13th when it again changed to the eastward.

18 June 1788

At six o'clock in the morning of the 18th they saw an island right a-head, bearing north half west eight or nine miles distant: they sounded when about six miles from the land, but got no bottom with sixty fathoms of line; at this time Captain Marshall perceived several canoes with their sails set, and two or three men in each canoe, coming towards the ship, but they presently put back again and made for the shore. This island is very low and level, and extends north-east, and south-west, terminating at each end in a low, flat point, with an appearance of a large bay in the middle; the Captain named it Hopper's Island; it is situated in 00° 03' south latitude, and 173° 43' longitude east from Greenwich.

At seven o'clock they saw another island smaller than the former, lying about six miles to the south-west of Hopper's Island, and nearly the same in appearance; this was named Henderville's Island. Towards noon, another island made its appearance, which Captain Marshall named Woodle's Island, situated three miles to the north-west of Henderville's Island. Five large canoes with sails set put off from Woodle's Island, and came towards the ship, but when about four miles distant, they turned back and stood for the shore. The wind blowing off the land prevented them from getting in with the shore, so as to enable them to give a particular description of these islands; they seemed to abound with cocoa-nut, and a variety of other trees. At three o'clock in the afternoon, the *Scarborough* being within three miles of Henderville's Island, they sounded with sixty fathoms of line, but got no ground. Several large fires were lighted up on the shore, and the natives assembled in vast numbers on the beach, many of them pointing at the ship with looks of wonder and surprise; presently afterwards, nineteen canoes, with five or six men in each, came off from the shore and made towards the ship, on which Captain Marshall lay to, in hopes they would come along side; several of them came within a quarter of a mile of the ship, and then taking down their sails, they stopt to gaze at the vessel, but nothing would induce them to come alongside; however, as more canoes were seen coming from the island, Captain Marshall determined to lay to till they all returned on shore, as there was a probability of his procuring some refreshments from them: two of the last canoes made for the ship without the least hesitation; on this, the Captain ordered his people out of sight that the natives might not be intimidated. When the canoes were close to the ship, the Indians began to talk, and made signs for them to bring the ship nearer the island.

After talking with the natives some time, the Captain shewed them a few small nails, a quart bottle, and a looking-glass, all of which they seemed very desirous to obtain; however, they could not be prevailed on to bring their canoes along-side, but three of them jumped out and swam to the ship; a rope was given them to take hold of, but they could not be persuaded to come on board. On receiving their little presents they laughed very heartily, and by way of exchange gave the Captain some beads and teeth of beasts or animals, which they wore about their necks as ornaments: this circumstance serves to show that they have some idea of barter.

After making signs a second time for them to bring the ship nearer the island, they took their leave, and presently afterwards all the canoes returning towards the shore, Captain Marshall made sail and stood to the northward. The situation of these islands has already been mentioned, they lie in nearly a north-west and south-east direction: Hopper's Island appears to be about ten leagues in length, Henderville's Island six leagues, and Woodle's Island the same.

It is to be lamented that Captain Marshall had not an opportunity of surveying these islands more minutely, as there is scarcely a doubt of their affording a variety of refreshments; for though nothing of the kind was seen in the canoes, yet the natives were plump and fleshy, and seemed to live at their ease: there is also an appearance of a most excellent harbour at Hopper's Island.

The inhabitants seem to be a fine set of people; they are of a copper colour, stout and well made; their hair is long and black, with black eyes and eye brows, and they seem to have very fine teeth. The only ornaments seen amongst them were necklaces made of beads intermixed with teeth, and many of them had their faces painted white.

A Canoe and Natives of Mulgrave's Range

If we may judge of these people from the construction of their canoes, they certainly possess a considerable share of contrivance and ingenuity: many of them are large enough to contain sixteen or twenty people; they are narrow, and built to sail very fast, yet there is not the least danger of their oversetting, as they are steadied with an out-rigger resembling a ladder on the weather side, to one end of which a log of wood is fastened, cut sharp at each end in the form of a boat; this not only serves to keep the canoe upright, but likewise holds her to windward. At the other end of the out-rigger, a stout rope is fixed, which leads up to the mast head and serves as a shroud; and when the wind blows fresh, two or more men, according to the size of the canoe, go out upon the ladder to keep her upright.

Though these canoes always sail on the same side, yet they are so contrived as to sail one way as well as the other, and the Indians manage them with such dexterity that they put about much sooner than our boats. Every canoe has a sail, which in general is very large; they appear to be made of raw-silk, neatly sewed together, and are cut in the form of our shoulder of mutton sail, with a yard at the fore-leach, and another at the foot, so that when they want to put their canoe about, they only have to shift their tack and bring it to leeward of the mast: in short, from what little Captain Marshall saw of these people, they appeared to be lively, ingenious and expert.

20 June 1788

After quitting these new discovered Islands, Captain Marshall stood to the northward, with a light breeze at east north-east, and at five o'clock in the morning of the 20th, they saw an island bearing east north-east, eight miles distant; it appeared very low, and almost level with the water, so that when only four miles distant they could perceive nothing but trees. When Captain Marshall got close in with the land, he found it to be a chain of islands, extending from south-east to north-west for the distance of more than thirty leagues. Having a favourable breeze, they run along the islands about three miles from shore, and several canoes with sails set, came after the ship, but none of them would come near her. Great numbers of the natives presently assembled on the beach, in order to gratify their curiosity in looking at the ship; this induced Captain Marshall to lay to in expectation of the natives coming along-side, but not one of them ventured near the ship: at one time he had an intention of sending his boat on shore in order to procure some refreshments, as many of his crew were laid up with the scurvy; however, he prudently declined taking this step, as it certainly would have been hazarding too much to have sent a few men amongst an ignorant multitude, with whose temper and disposition they were perfectly unacquainted.

The centre of these islands is situated in 1° 50' north latitude, 173° 00' east longitude. They are very low, and yet it is rather remarkable, that on sounding, when not more than a mile from the land, there was no bottom found with eighty fathoms of line. Within the islands there appeared to be some fine harbours, and they probably afford a variety of refreshments. The natives seemed to be nearly black, and their canoes were constructed much in the same manner as those already described.

22 June 1788

There being no prospect of procuring any refreshments from these people, Captain Marshall made sail, and at noon on the 22d they saw land in the direction of north by east, eight miles distant; it appeared very low, flat, and full of trees. By four o'clock, they were close in with the southernmost land, and saw a great number of canoes sailing close to the shore, some of which came towards the ship, and two of them very near, but nothing would entice them to come along-side. The people appeared much the same as those at Henderville's Island, and their canoes were of a similar construction; one of them had a kind of vane at the mast head, which appeared to be made of the same materials as their sail. In running along shore, they found it to consist of six different islands, extending from north by east to south by west, to the length of fourteen or fifteen leagues; the centre of them is situated in 2° 58' north latitude, and 173° 00' east longitude. The southernmost island, Captain Marshall named Allen's Island; the second, Gillespy's Island; the third, Touching's Island; the fourth, Clarke's Island; the fifth, Smith's Island; and the northernmost, *Scarborough* Island. They ran along these islands about three miles distant from the land, and kept the lead constantly going, but could get no bottom, which appeared rather extraordinary as the land is very low. There appears to be good anchorage between these islands, and the water very smooth, and they seem to abound with cocoa-nut and cabbage trees. By the time they were abreast of *Scarborough* Island, it grew so dark that they could not see the land; luckily, however, the Indians lighted two very large fires which enabled them to get entirely clear of all the islands.

23 June 1788

At six o'clock in the afternoon of the 23d, more land made its appearance, bearing north to north-west, four leagues distant, but night coming on, they tacked and stood to the southward.

24 June 1788

By two o'clock the next day, they were within two miles of the land, and found it to be a chain of islands, extending from east to nearly west for more than twenty-five leagues; and they perceived a reef from the easternmost point of land, which ran at least three leagues into the sea. The shore on the north-west side of these islands is bold and steep; the *Scarborough* coasted along within a mile of the land, and frequently sounded with an hundred fathoms of line, but could get no bottom; at the same time they saw the water break near the shore, and a vast number of the natives were collected on the beach. About three o'clock, a small canoe with two men in her came off from the shore, on which Captain Marshall hove to, in order to give them an opportunity of coming up with the ship, but when they were about one hundred yards from the vessel, they put back again as fast as possible, seemingly very much frightened: these men had skins wrapped round their waists, and their hair was ornamented with shells and beads. After they left the ship, Captain Marshall made sail, being desirous to make the westward part of the islands if possible before the night came on; but in this he was disappointed, as the wind grew light and baffling. Several large canoes now put off from the shore with eight or ten men in each; it already has been observed that the *Charlotte*, Captain Gilbert, was in company with the *Scarborough*; at this time she was some distance a-stern, and the canoes all went along-side her; several of them went on board the *Charlotte*, and ran fore and aft, stealing every thing that lay in their way; one of them in particular, got hold of the pump-break, and attempted to jump over-board with it, but was stopped by one of the sailors. They appeared to be very civilized, and all of them had coverings round the waist: their ornaments were necklaces made of beads, to which a cross was suspended, in the same manner as those worn by the Spaniards.

25 June 1788-27 June 1788

Captain Marshall distinguished these islands by the name of Lord Mulgrave's Islands, in honour of the Right Honourable Lord Mulgrave. The southernmost of them is situated in 5° 58' north latitude, and 172° 3' east longitude, and the northernmost in 6° 29' north latitude, and 171° 10' east longitude. At noon on the 25th, they got round the westernmost island, and thought themselves entirely clear of them all, as the day was very fair, and no land could be seen from the mast-head; at the same time they had a long swell: on this, Captain Marshall stood on under an easy sail during the night, but was very much surprised at daylight the next morning to see land on the weather quarter, and a large island on the lee quarter, between which they must have passed in the night, and certainly very near that on their lee, though they sounded every half hour, but never struck the ground. Lord Mulgrave's Islands abound with cocoa-nut-trees, and they could perceive remnants of oranges and various other sorts of fruit, although the natives offered nothing of the sort to barter. These islanders had not any offensive weapons whatever, so that they probably are on very friendly terms with each other. With a light easterly breeze, they kept their course to the northward, and at noon on the 27th, in 7° 25' north latitude, and 171° 10' east longitude, they saw land bearing from north by east to north north-west. Having now a fresh breeze, Captain Marshall run in with the land, and found it to be a cluster of small islands lying east and west of each other, but no appearance was seen of their being inhabited.

28 June 1788

At noon on the 28th, more islands were seen, bearing from north to north-west by west, three or four leagues distant, their latitude at that time was 8° 02' north, and 170° 57' east longitude. The weather being very hazy, with constant rain, they wore, and stood from the land; however, the afternoon proving tolerably clear, they again stood towards it, and by four o'clock were close in with the westernmost island. Two large canoes were lying on a sandy beach, but they did not perceive any inhabitants. At five o'clock they saw several more islands, bearing north north-east, five or six leagues distant. During the night, Captain Marshall stood under an easy sail, and at day-light the next morning land was seen a-head bearing north by east six leagues, and some land bearing east seventeen leagues distant. These islands, like all they had yet seen, were very low, and entirely covered with lofty trees; on sounding, they got no ground with an hundred fathoms of line. Their latitude at noon was 8° 59' north, and 170° 24' east longitude.

30 June 1788

At five in the afternoon, more islands were seen, bearing north, five leagues distant, but night coming on they wore and stood to the southward. In the forenoon of the 30th, they ran between two islands, about five leagues distant from each other, and surrounded by a number of breakers: by eleven o'clock they were entirely clear of all the land. Their observation at noon gave 9° 34' north latitude, and the longitude was 169° 22' east. These last islands were supposed by Captain Marshall to be those which Lord Anson discovered, and named Barbadoes Islands.

31 July 1788

Having now a clear navigation, they prosecuted their voyage without meeting with any thing worthy of notice till the 31st of July, when at six clock in the morning they saw the island of Saypan bearing west by south six leagues distant. Having light baffling winds, they did not get in with the land till the approach of evening, so that the night was spent in standing off and on. At day-light the next morning, Captain Marshall sent his boat on shore, with the chief mate and four seamen, to procure some refreshments, and look for anchorage. At two o'clock in the afternoon, the boats returned loaded with cocoa-nuts and cabbage, both, as the men reported, from the same tree, but they could find no place for a vessel to anchor in, the water being very deep close to the land, with a rocky bottom, and so heavy a surf that the boat did not land without great difficulty. Not meeting with a harbour at Sapan, the Captain determined to make the best of his way to Tinian, where he might come to anchor and get his sick people on shore, having no less than fifteen men laid up with the scurvy, and the rest of his crew were so weak that they could scarcely work the ship: the wind, however, was so variable, that they did not reach the south-west side of that island till afternoon on the 4th, when they anchored in twenty-five fathoms water, and soon afterwards the *Charlotte* came to anchor a small distance from the *Scarborough*.

5 August 1788-8 August 1788

Early the next morning, Captain Marshall sent his sick people on shore, with a tent, and a sufficient quantity of provisions to serve them five days. After landing the sick, and erecting their tent, the boats crew walked about the island, and saw a great number of cattle, hogs, and fowls, but they only caught a calf, one hog, and a fowl or two, and loaded the boat with cocoanuts, oranges, and limes. On the 6th, the chief mate was sent on shore to look for fresh water; he soon found out the well, mentioned in Lord Anson's voyage, but it was quite dry, and there was not any fresh water to be met with within two miles of the landing place. The boat returned at noon, loaded with fruit of different sorts. Toward evening the wind came round to south south-west blowing very strong, which sent a heavy sea rolling into the bay, and occasioned the *Scarborough* to pitch very much. The wind still blowing strongly into the bay, Captain Marshall sent his boat on shore on the 7th, to bring off the sick people, which they accomplished with much danger and difficulty; in the mean time, every thing was got ready for sea, the Captain being determined to get away the moment the wind shifted to south or south by east, so that they could clear the west part of the island. During the night, they had so heavy a gale at south-west that they expected every minute to be driven on shore; fortunately, however, at day-break, the wind shifted to south south-east, on which they immediately cut the cable and ran clear of the land: Captain Gilbert cut both his cables and followed the *Scarborough*. Scarce had they cleared the land before the wind again shifted to south-south-west, and blew a complete hurricane, so that had the vessels then been at anchor, they must inevitably have been driven on shore. Though Captain Marshall's people were on land so short a time, they found amazing benefit from it, their strength gradually returned, and soon afterwards they were perfectly restored to health.

7 September 1788

No particular occurrence happened during their passage from Tinian to China; they saw the Lema Islands in the afternoon of the 7th of September, and came to anchor in Macao Roads the following afternoon.

Chapter XXII.

Supplemental Account of Animals

BIRDS.

No. 139. **BANKIAN COCKATOO.** Order II. Pies. Genus V. Parrot.

This is about the size of the great white cockatoo; the length twenty-two inches. The bill is exceedingly short, and of a pale lead-colour. The head feathers are pretty long, so as to enable the bird to erect them into a crest at will: The colour of the head, neck, and under parts of the body are dusky brown, inclining to olive, darkest on the belly: the feathers of the top of the head and back part of the neck are edged with olive; the rest of the plumage on the upper part of the body, the wings, and tail, are of a glossy black; the last is pretty long and a little rounded at the end; the two middle feathers are wholly black; the others of a fine vermilion in the middle for about one-third, otherwise black; the outer edge of the exterior feather black the whole length. Legs black.

This bird was met with in New South Wales, and is supposed to be a variety, if not a different sex, from the Bankian Cockatoo described in the General Synopsis of Birds, Supplement, p. 63. pl. 109. It varies, however, in not having the feathers of the head or those of the wing-coverts marked with buff-coloured spots; nor is the red part of the tail crossed with black bars, as in that bird.

With the above specimen was sent the head of another, which differed in having a mixture of yellow in various parts of it. We have been informed, that the red part of the tail in this last is barred with black, not unlike that described by Mr. Latham in the Synopsis. From these circumstances, it may be presumed, that this bird is subject to great variety.

Bankian Cockatoo

RED SHOULDERED PARROT. Order II. Pies. Genus V.

This bird is about the size of the Guinea Parrakeet. Total length ten inches and a half: the general colour of the plumage is green, inclining to yellow on the under parts: the top of the head, the outer edge of the wing, and some parts of the middle of the same are deep blue: all round the base of the bill crimson, with a mixture of the same on the fore part of the neck, but between the bill and eye is a mixture of yellow: the shoulders, and under parts of the wings are blood red: two or three of the inner quills, and the vent pale red: the greater quills dusky, fringed outwardly with yellow: the tail is greatly wedged in shape, the feathers at the base chesnut, towards the end dull blue: the bill and legs are brown.

This species inhabits New South Wales; and we believe it to be hitherto non-descript.

Red Shouldered Parrakeet

CRESTED GOAT SUCKER. Order III. Passerine. Genus XLV.

This bird is somewhat smaller than our European species, measuring only nine inches and a half in length. The general colour of the plumage on the upper parts is dark-brown, mottled and crossed with obscure whitish bars: the quills are plain brown, but five or six of the outer ones marked with dusky white spots on the outer webs: the tail is rounded in shape, and marked with twelve narrow bars of a dusky white, mottled with black, as are the various whitish marks on the upper parts: the under parts of the body are more or less white; but the fore part of the neck and breast are crossed with numerous dusky bars: the bill is black, but the gape and within yellow; the sides of the mouth furnished with bristles, as in other goat-suckers; besides which, at the base of the bill are ten or twelve erect stiff bristles, thinly barbed on their sides, and standing perfectly upright as a crest, giving the bird a singular appearance: the legs are weak, longer than in most of the tribe, and of a pale yellow colour; claws brown.

New Holland Goat-sucker

NEW HOLLAND CASSOWARY. Order VI. Struthious. Genus LIX. Cassowary.

This is a species differing in many particulars from that generally known, and is a much larger bird, standing higher on its legs, and having the neck longer than in the common one. Total length seven feet two inches. The bill is not greatly different from that of the common Cassowary; but the horny appendage, or helmet on the top of the head, in this species is totally wanting: the whole of the head and neck is also covered with feathers, except the throat and fore part of the neck about half way, which are not so well feathered as the rest; whereas in the common Cassowary, the head and neck are bare and carunculated as in the turkey.

The plumage in general consists of a mixture of brown and grey, and the feathers are somewhat curled or bent at the ends in the natural state: the wings are so very short as to be totally useless for flight, and indeed, are scarcely to be distinguished from the rest of the plumage, were it not for their standing out a little. The long spines which are seen in the wings of the common sort, are in this not observable,--nor is there any appearance of a tail. The legs are stout, formed much as in the Galeated Cassowary, with the addition of their being jagged or sawed the whole of their length at the back part.

This bird is not uncommon in New Holland, as several of them have been seen about Botany Bay, and other parts. The one from which the plate was taken, was shot within two miles of the settlement at Sydney Cove, and the drawing made on the spot by Lieutenant Watts. The skin being sent over to England in spirits, has been put into attitude, and is now the property of Sir Joseph Banks, to whom it was presented by Lord Sydney. Although this bird cannot fly, it runs so swiftly, that a greyhound can scarcely overtake it. The flesh is said to be in taste not unlike beef.

New Holland Cassowary
WHITE GALLINULE. Order VII. Cloven-footed. Genus LXXV.

This beautiful bird greatly resembles the purple Gallinule in shape and make, but is much superior in size, being as large as a dunghil fowl. The length from the end of the bill to that of the claws is two feet three inches: the bill is very stout, and the colour of it, the whole of the top of the head, and the irides red; the sides of the head round the eyes are reddish, very thinly sprinkled with white feathers; the whole of the plumage without exception is white. The legs the colour of the bill.

This species is pretty common on Lord Howe's Island, Norfolk Island, and other places, and is a very tame species. The other sex, supposed to be the male, is said to have some blue on the wings.

White Gallinule
DOG OF NEW SOUTH WALES.
Genus XII. Canis.--Lin. Syst. Nat.
Genus XVII. Dog.--Penn. Hist. Quad.

The height of this species, standing erect, is rather less than two feet: the length two feet and a half. The head is formed much like that of a fox, the ears short and erect, with whiskers from one to two inches in length on the muzzle. The general colour of the upper parts is pale brown, growing lighter towards the belly: the hind part of the fore legs, and the fore part of the hinder ones white, as are the feet of both: the tail is of a moderate length, somewhat bushy, but in a less degree than that of the fox: the teeth are much the same as is usual in the genus, as may be seen in the top of the plate where the animal is represented.

This species inhabits New South Wales. The specimen from which the annexed plate was taken, (a female) is now alive in the possession of the Marchioness of Salisbury, at Hatfield-House, and was sent over as a present to Mr. Nepean, from Governor Phillip. It has much of the manners of the dog, but is of a very savage nature, and not likely to change in this particular. It laps like other dogs, but neither barks nor growls if vexed and teized; instead of which, it erects the hairs of the whole body like bristles, and seems furious: it is very eager after its prey, and is fond of rabbits or chickens, raw, but will not touch dressed meat. From its fierceness and agility it has greatly the advantage of other animals much superior in size; for a very fine French fox-dog being put to it, in a moment it seized him by the loins, and would have soon put an end to his existence, had not help been at hand. With the utmost ease it is able to leap over the back of an ass, and was very near worrying one to death, having fastened on it, so that the creature was not able to disengage himself without assistance; it has been also known to run down both deer and sheep.

A second of these is in the possession of Mr. Lascelles, of which we have received much the same account in respect to its ferocity; whence it is scarcely to be expected that this elegant animal will ever become familiar.

Dog of New South Wales
SPOTTED MARTIN.
Genus XV. Mustela.--Lin. Syst. Nat.
Genus XXIII. Weesel.--Penn. Hist. Quad.

The species is about the size of a large polecat, and measures from the tip of the nose to the setting on of the tail eighteen inches; the tail itself being nearly the same length. The visage is pointed in shape, and the whole make of the animal does not ill resemble that of the Fossane. The general colour of the fur is black, marked all over with irregular blotches of white, the tail not excepted, which has an elegant appearance, and tapers gradually to a point.

The situation of the teeth and jaws is much the same as in the rest of the genus, as may be seen in the upper part of the plate.

Inhabits the neighbourhood of Port Jackson.

Martin Cat
KANGUROO RAT.
Genus XVII. Didelphis.--Lin. Syst. Nat.
Genus XXII. Opossum.--Penn. Hist. 2uad.

The upper jaw of this species has two cutting teeth in front, with three others on each side of them, and at a distance one false grinder, sharp at the edge, and channelled, or fluted, on the sides, and close to these, two true grinders: in the lower jaw are two long cutting teeth, formed like those of the squirrel, with three grinders, corresponding with those in the upper jaw.

The general shape of the body is not widely different from that of the Kanguroo, both in respect to the shortness of the fore legs and the peculiar construction of the hind ones; but the visage being strongly similar to that of the rat, and the colour of the whole not ill resembling that animal, it has obtained the name of the Kanguroo Rat.

This is an inhabitant of New Holland, and two of the species are now to be seen alive at the curious exhibition of animals over Exeter Exchange. One of these, being a female, has brought forth young, one of which is represented in the same plate with the adult animal. On the upper part of the same plate is figured the jaw of a full grown subject.

Kanguroo Rat
THE LACED LIZARD. Genus CXXII. Lacerta.--Lin. Sist. Nat.

This most elegant species is in length, from the nose to the end of the tail, about forty inches: in the mouth are a few weak teeth, though rather sharp, at about a quarter of an inch distance one from another: the tongue is long and forked: the general shape is slender; and the ground colour of the skin, on the upper parts, a brownish or bluish black, whimsically marked with golden yellow; in some parts this colour is beautifully mottled or freckled, like some kinds of lace-work; in others, striped in various directions, particularly on the legs, which seem as if striped across with black and white: the under parts are yellow, crossed with single bars of black on the chin and throat, and double clouded ones on the belly: the toes are five in number on each foot, barred across with black and yellow, as the legs, and each furnished with a crooked black claw: the tail measures more in length than the whole of the body; towards the base, clouded and marked as the rest; but the further half banded with black and yellow, each band three inches broad, the end running to a very sharp point.

This beautiful Lizard is not uncommon at Port Jackson, where it is reputed a harmless species. Individuals vary much one from another, in respect to the length of the tail, as also in the colour of the markings; some having those parts marked with a pure silvery white, which in the above described are yellow.

Laced Lizard
BAG-THROATED BALISTES. Genus CXXXV. Balistes.--Lin. Syst. Nat.

The size of the fish figured in the plate is uncertain, as we have only obtained a drawing of it without any description.--It agrees in many things with others of the genus, and does not greatly differ from one figured in Willughby's Icthyologia, Tab. 1. 22. but has the body longer in proportion. The erect horn or spine is placed over, and a little behind the eyes, as in Willughby's figure, attended with two shorter ones directly behind the first: the long spine is quite straight, sharp at the point, and deeply sawed on the back part. Another singularity presents itself in this species, which is, a deep pouch-like appendage beneath the throat, in shape not unlike what is called Hippocrates's sleeve, or rather a jelly bag.

This fish is found pretty commonly on the coast of New South Wales, and was called by the sailors the Old Wife, having much resemblance in many things to the species so named. When skinned, it was thought pretty good eating.

68

A fish of New South Wales
A FISH OF NEW SOUTH WALES.

Of this fish it can only be said, that the ground colour is much the same as that of our mackarel, marked with several round, blue and white spots; and that, in the plate, it is represented faithfully from a drawing by Daniel Butler sent from New South Wales, where it is in great plenty, and is thought to taste much like a dolphin. As to the genus, it is difficult to say with certainty to which it belongs, as it is deficient in the characteristics of those generally known; it is therefore left to the reader to settle this matter according to his own opinion.

Fish of New South Wales
PORT JACKSON SHARK. Genus CXXXI. Squalus.--Lin. Syst. Nat.

The length of the specimen from which the drawing was taken, is two feet; and it is about five inches and an half over at the broadest part, from thence tapering to the tail: the skin is rough, and the colour, in general, brown, palest on the under parts: over the eyes on each side is a prominence, or long ridge, of about three inches; under the middle of which the eyes are placed: the teeth are very numerous, there being at least ten or eleven rows; the forward teeth are small and sharp, but as they are placed more backward, they become more blunt and larger, and several rows are quite flat at top, forming a kind of bony palate, somewhat like that of the Wolf-fish; differing, however, in shape, being more inclined to square than round, which they are in that fish: the under jaw is furnished much in the same manner as the upper: the breathing holes are five in number, as is usual in the genus: on the back are two fins, and before each stands a strong spine, much as in the Prickly Hound, or Dog, fish: it has also two pectoral, and two ventral fins; but besides these, there is likewise an anal fin, placed at a middle distance between the last and the tail: the tail itself, is as it were divided, the upper part much longer than the under.

At first sight, the above might be taken for the Prickly Hound-fish, or Squalus Spinax of Linnoeus, of which a good figure may be seen in Willughby's Icthyol. Tab. B. 5. f. 1, but it differs, first, in having the prominent ridge over the eyes, of a great length; secondly, in the formation of the teeth; thirdly, in having an anal fin, of which the Prickly Hound is destitute; all these circumstances concur to prove it a new species.

This was taken at Port Jackson, but to what size it may usually arrive cannot be determined; perhaps not to a great one, as the teeth appear very complete. Some sharks, however, of an enormous size have been seen and caught thereabouts, though of what sort cannot here be determined.

Port Jackson Shark
WATTS'S SHARK. Genus CXXXI. Squalus.--Lin. Syst.

This, we believe, is a species which has hitherto escaped the researches of our Icthyologists. The length of the specimen is nineteen inches: the head is broad, and angular in shape; but the body rounded, and nearly equal in its dimensions for above half the length, when it suddenly grows very small, and so continues to the end of the tail: the colour of the body is brown in different shades, and there are three rows of large pale spots, of an irregular shape, most of them dark within; one row passes down the middle, the others are on each side; besides which there are others below them less conspicuous. The mouth is placed nearer the end of the head than in most of the genus, and furnished in the front with nine sharp crooked teeth, in three rows, and a great number of small ones on each side. The eyes project considerably above the rest of the head, and are placed on the upper part of it; the space between is hollowed or sunk in: at the most forward part of the head are two cartilaginous appendages, jagged at the end, with four others, nearly similar, on each side between the first and the breathing holes: the pectoral fins are placed beneath these last; the abdominal about the middle of the body; and the anal, more than half way between the last and the tail; besides which, the under part is finned from that place to the end: on the upper part of the body are two fins, both placed uncommonly far back, as in the figure.

This fish was met with in Sydney Cove, Port Jackson, by Lieutenant Watts, and is supposed to be full as voracious as any of the genus, in proportion to its size; for after having lain on the deck for two hours, seemingly quiet, on Mr. Watts's dog passing by, the shark sprung upon it with all the ferocity imaginable, and seized it by the leg; nor could the dog have disengaged himself had not the people near at hand come to his assistance.

Watt's Shark
GREAT BROWN KINGSFISHER.--Lath. Syn. ii. p. 603, No. 1.
Order II. Pies. Genus XXIII. Kingsfisher.

69

The length of this species is from sixteen to eighteen inches: the bill, three inches and an half, or even more; the upper mandible is brown, and the under white, but brown at the base: the head is pretty full of feathers, sufficiently so to form a crest when erected; the colour whitish, and most of the feathers either tipped or crossed with black: the neck and under parts of the body are much the same in colour, crossed on the sides with dusky lines: over the forehead the colour is dusky brown, almost black, passing backwards in an irregular shaped streak a good way behind the eye: the back, and major part of the wing, is black or dusky, but the middle of the wing is of a glossy blue-green, as is also the lower part of the back and rump: the tail is barred with pale rust-colour and black, inclining to purple, and towards the end whitish: the legs are of a dusky yellow, the claws are black.

These birds vary much, the colours being more or less brilliant, and in some of them the tail is wholly barred with white and black, and the legs brown or blackish.

This species inhabits various places in the South Seas, being pretty common at New Guinea; but the specimen from which our figure was taken, was sent from Port Jackson in South Wales, where, likewise, it is not unfrequently met with. We believe it has not yet been figured in any British work.

Great brown Kingsfisher
KANGUROO.

This very curious animal being naturally an object of particular curiosity, we are happy to be enabled, before this book is given to the world, to correct some errors which had crept into our account and representation of it. In page 149 it is stated, that the Kanguroo has four teeth (by which were meant cutting teeth) in the upper jaw, opposed to two in the under. The truth is, that there are six opposed to two, as may be perceived in the engraved representation of the skeleton of a Kanguroo's head, inserted at page 168. The same arrangement of teeth takes place in the Opossum, described in that page, which is there, still more erroneously, said to have only two cutting teeth opposed to two. This latter mistake arose from the difficulty of examining the mouth of the living animal. It is since dead, and the teeth are found to be disposed as now stated, and as represented in the scull of the Vulpine Opossum, in the same plate with that of the Kanguroo.

But the most important error is in the position of the Kanguroo, as represented in our plate at page 106. The true standing posture of the Kanguroo is exactly the same as that of the Kanguroo Rat, delineated at page 277; namely, with the rump several inches from the ground, (in large specimens, not less than eight) and resting entirely on the long last joint of the hinder legs, the whole under side of which is bare and callous like a hoof. This mistake was occasioned merely by the adherence of the engraver to the drawing from which he worked; which, among others, came from Mr. White, the surgeon at Port Jackson: too implicit reliance being placed on an authority which, in this respect, turned out delusive.

With respect to the representations of the Kanguroo which have hitherto been published, it may be observed, that nothing is wanting to that in Captain Cook's first voyage, except the character of the toes of the hinder legs, and in particular the distinguishing of a minute, but very characteristic circumstance, in the inner claw of each, which is divided down the middle into two, as if split by some sharp instrument. The same remark is applicable to the plate in Mr. Pennant's History of Quadrupeds, which appears to have been copied from the other. Mr. Pennant was the first author who gave a scientific description of the Kanguroo, in his History of Quadrupeds, p. 306. No. 184. and of the New Holland Opossum, p. 310. No. 188.

Zimmerman, in his Zoologia Geographica, p. 527, confounds the Kanguroo with the great Jerboa of Africa, described by Allamand, in his additions to Buffon; and by Mr. Pennant, History of Quadrupeds, p. 432. No. 293.

Our own plate of the Kanguroo very accurately expresses the form and character of that animal, and is deficient only in the position, which unfortunately was not remarked till the plate was worked off, and the book almost ready for delivery.

ANECDOTE OF CAPTAIN COOK AND O'TOO.

As nothing can be devoid of interest which relates to a man so justly admired as Captain Cook, the reader will probably be pleased to find here, though out of its proper place, an anecdote communicated by Mr. Webber. It exhibits in a pleasing point of view the friendship which subsisted between that great navigator and the Otaheitean chief O'too, a circumstance highly to the honour of both; since it displays in them the power of discerning real merit, though obscured by diversity of manners, and that of being able to impress a steady attachment, where nothing more was to be expected than transient regard. Under every species of disparity, goodness of heart supplies both a medium of attraction, and an indissoluble bond of union.

Every reader must have seen with pleasure the charming proof of O'too's tender and inviolable friendship for Captain Cook, which appears in page 233 of this work; where he is described as attended by a man carrying the portrait of that illustrious Englishman, without which he never moves from one place to another. That portrait, as Mr. Webber assures us, was obtained in the following manner.

O'too, by the Captain's particular desire, sat to Mr. Webber, in order to furnish such a memorial of his features, as might serve for the subject of a complete whole length picture, on the return of the ship to England. When the portrait was finished, and O'too was informed that no more sittings would be necessary, he anxiously enquired of Captain Cook, and Captain Clerke, what might be the particular meaning and purpose of this painting. He was informed, that it would be kept by Captain Cook, as a perpetual memorial of his person, his friendship, and the many favours received from him. He seemed pleased with the idea, and instantly replied, that, for the very same reasons, a picture of Captain Cook would be highly acceptable to him. This answer, so unexpected, and expressed with strong tokens of real attachment, made both Captain Clerke and Mr. Webber his advocates; and Captain Cook, charmed with the natural sincerity of his manner, complied with his request much more readily than on any other occasion he would have granted such a favour.

When the portrait was finished it was framed, and with a box, lock, and key, by which it was secured, was delivered to O'too; who received it with inexpressible satisfaction. He readily, and, as the event has proved, most faithfully promised that he would preserve it always with the utmost care; and would show it to the commanders of such ships as might in future touch at the Society Islands. Who can fail to love a character like that of O'too, in which unalterable steadiness of affection is as conspicuous, as honest and natural ardour? Long may he enjoy his authority and his health; and preserve the honourable memorial of his friend, without being afflicted by the knowledge of that melancholy catastrophe which terminated the career of his glory!

With respect to the yellow gum, or resin, mentioned in page 60, we are informed by Dr. Blane, physician to St. Thomas's Hospital, that he has found it remarkably efficacious in the cure of old fluxes; and this not only in a few instances, but in many obstinate cases. Of the plants in general which have been brought from Botany Bay, and the adjacent country, no notice has been taken in this work, as it would have led to such a detail as must too considerably have extended its limits. Many of them are now to be seen in the highest perfection at the nursery gardens of that eminent and learned botanist, Mr. Lee, of Hammersmith: who still retains enough of zeal for his favourite science, to regret that the discovery of those countries was not made at a period of his life, when he could have gone personally to reap the glorious harvest they afford.

The following account of the weather in Botany Bay and Port Jackson, communicated by Lieutenant Watts, may perhaps be found important.

During the seven days we were in Botany Bay the weather was generally fine, and very warm. The thermometer on a mean stood at 78°. it never exceeded 80°. and one day, which was thick and rainy, the wind blowing strongly from the south, it fell to 63°. In Port Jackson the weather was at first much the same, but afterwards, the days became very hot, and the nights constantly brought on tremendous thunder, lightning, and rain. The thermometer, at eleven o'clock in the forenoon, was generally about 80°. but when the sea breezes set in it usually fell two or three degrees. One very sultry day was felt soon after the arrival of the fleet. The thermometer, on board, stood at 88°. and on shore, though in the shade, at 92°. On the 15th of March was a terrible squall of wind, accompanied by thunder, lightning, and rain. The thermometer then fell from 80° to 50°. and in other squalls it frequently fell 15 or 20 degrees.

Such are the principal notices hitherto received from the new settlement on the southern continent, which, if from unavoidable circumstances, they are a little deficient in point of order, will, it is hoped, make ample amends by their novelty, importance, and authenticity.

BLACK FLYING OPOSSUM.

Genus XVII. Didelphis. Lin. Syst. Nat.
Genus XXII. Opossum. Penn. Hist. Quad.

The following is, according to every appearance, a new animal of this genus. The length from the tip of the nose, which is pointed in shape, to the root of the tail, is twenty inches; of the tail itself twenty-two inches, at the base quite light, increasing gradually to black at the end: the width across the loins sixteen inches: the ears are large and erect: the coat or fur is of a much richer texture or more delicate than the sea-otter of Cook's River: on the upper parts of the body, at first sight, appearing of a glossy black, but on a nicer inspection, is really what the French call

71

petit gris, or minever, being mixed with grey; the under parts are white, and on each hip may be observed a tan-coloured spot, nearly as big as a shilling; at this part the fur is thinnest, but at the root of the tail it is so rich and close that the hide cannot be felt through it. The fur is also continued to the claws: the membrane, which is expanded on each side of the body, is situated much as in the grey species, though broader in proportion. The jaws are furnished with teeth, placed as in some others of this genus: in the upper jaw forwards are four small cutting teeth, then two canine ones, and backwards five grinders: the under jaw has two long large cutting teeth, like the Vulpine Opossum, [See skeleton on the plate at page 168.] five grinders, with no intermediate canine ones, the space being quite vacant. The fore legs have five toes on each foot, with a claw on each; the hinder ones four toes, with claws, (the three outside ones without any separation) and a thumb without a claw, enabling the animal to use the foot as a hand, as many of the opossum tribe are observed to do. See the skeleton of the foot in the annexed plate.

This beautiful quadruped inhabits New South Wales. The specimen from which the above account has been taken, is a male, and the property of Henry Constantine Nowell, Esq. of Shiplake, in Oxfordshire. The fur of it is so beautiful, and of so rare a texture, that should it hereafter be found in plenty, it might probably be thought a very valuable article of commerce.

Black flying Opossum

APPENDIX

Table I. Route of the *Alexander*, Lieutenant Shortland, from the Cape of Good Hope to Botany Bay
Table II. Route of the *Supply*, Lieut. Ball, after parting with the *Alexander*, to Botany Bay
Table III. Route of the *Supply*, Lieut. Ball, from Port Jackson to Norfolk Island
Table IV. Route of the *Supply* from Norfolk Island to Port Jackson
Table V. Route of the *Supply* from Port Jackson to Lord Howe Island, and from thence to Port Jackson
Table VI. Route of the *Alexander*, Lieut. Shortland, from Port Jackson to Batavia
Table VII. Route of the *Lady Penrhyn*, Capt. Sever, from Port Jackson to Otaheite
Table VIII.Route of the *Lady Penrhyn*, Capt. Sever, from Otaheite to China
Table IX. Route of the *Scarborough*, Capt. Marshall, from Port Jackson to China

[The first page of the Tables of the Routes taken by ships of the First Fleet after leaving Port Jackson is reproduced above. A further 52 pages of such tables are not included in this ebook.]

A LIST OF CONVICTS SENT TO NEW SOUTH WALES, IN 1787. Name. Where Convicted. Date Of Conviction. Years. Abel, Robert London 23 Feb. 1785. 7 Abrams, Henry Abrahams, Esther London 30 August, 1786 7 Abell, Mary, alias Tilley Worcester 5 March, 1785 7 Acres, Thomas Exeter 14 March, 1786 7 Adams, John London 26 May, 1784 7 Adams, Mary Ditto 13 Decem. 1786 7 Agley, Richard Winchester 2 March, 1784 7 Allen, John Hertford 2 March, 1786 7 Allen, William Ormskirk 11 April, 1785 7 Allen, Charles London 7 July, 1784 7 Allen, Susannah Ditto 18 April, 1787 7 Allen, Mary Ditto 25 October, 1786 7 Allen, Jamasin, alias Boddington Ditto 25 Oct. 1786 7 Allen, Mary, alias Conner Ditto 10 Jan. 1787 7 Anderson, John Exeter 20 March, 1786 7 Anderson, Elizabeth London 10 Jan. 1787 7 Anderson, John Ditto 26 May, 1784 7 Anderson, Fanny Winchester 7 March, 1786 7 Archer, John London 26 May, 1784 7 Arscott, John Bodmin 18 August, 1783 7 Atkinson, George London 21 April, 1784 7 Ault, Sarah Ditto 21 Feb. 1787 7 Ayners, John, alias Agnew Ditto 26 May, 1784 7 Ayres John Ditto 21 April, 1784 7 Bartlett, James Winchester 1 March, 1785 7 Barsby, George Ditto 1 March, 1785 Life Barnett, Henry, alias Barnard, alias Burton Warwick 21 March, 1785 7 Bails, Robert Reading 28 Feb. 1785 Life Barnes, Stephen York 9 July, 1785 7 Bannister, George London 1 April, 1784 7 Barferd, John Ditto 14 Decem. 1784 7 Barland, George Ditto 7 July, 1784 7 Balding, James, alias William Ditto 23 Feb. 1785 7 Bason, Elizabeth, wife of William Bason New Sarum 24 July, 1784 7 Bayley, James Ditto 11 March, 1786 7 Bazley, John Exeter 12 Jan. 1785 7 Baker, Thomas Ditto 10 Jan. 1786 7 Barrett, Thomas Ditto 24 May, 1784 Life Batley, Caten Ditto 24 May, 1784 7 Barsby, Samuel Ditto 20 March, 1786 7 Ball, John Ditto 20 March, 1786 7 Barry, John Bristol 23 Novem. 1785 7 Barret, Daniel Barber, Elizabeth Baldwin, Ruth, alias Bowyer London 20 August, 1786 7 Baker, Martha Ditto 30 August, 1786 7 Bell, William Ditto 21 April, 1784 7 Benear, Samuel Ditto 26 May, 1784 7 Bellett, Jacob Ditto 12 Jan. 1785 7 Beardsley, Ann Derby 5 August, 1786 5 Best, John Beckford, Elizabeth London 10 Jan. 1787 7 Bellamy, Thomas Worcester 9 July, 1785 7 Bird, James Croydon 20 July, 1785 7 Bird, Samuel Ditto 20 July, 1785 7 Bishop, Joseph Bingham, John, alias Baughan Bingham, Elizabeth, alias

Mooring London Bird, Elizabeth, alias Winisred Maidstone 14 March, 1787 7 Blackhall, William Abingdon 6 March, 1786 7 Blunt, William London 10 Decem. 1783 7 Blake, Francis Ditto 26 May, 1784 7 Blatherhorn, William Exeter 24 May, 1784 Life Bloedworth, James Kingstone 3 Oct. 1785 7 Blanchett, Susannah Ditto 2 April, 1787 7 Bond, Peter London 23 Feb. 1785 7 Boyle, John London 23 Feb. 1785 7 Boggis, William Bond, William Exeter 18 July, 1785 7 Bond, Mary, wife of John Bond Wells 19 August, 1786 7 Boulton, Rebecca Lincoln 16 July, 1784 7 Bonner, Jane London 18 April, 1787 7 Bolton, Mary Shrewsbury 12 March, 1785 7 Brown, James Hertford 2 March, 1785 7 Brown, William Southwark 10 Jan. 1786 7 Brindley, John Warwick 21 March, 1785 7 Brown, Richard Reading 15 July, 1783 7 Brough, William Stafford 9 March, 1789 7 Bradley, James London 29 June, 1785 7 Bradley, James Ditto 6 May, 1784 7 Brown, Thomas Ditto 10 Septem. 1783 7 Bradbury, William Ditto 10 Septem. 1783 7 Bryant, Thomas Maidstone 15 March, 1784 7 Bryant, William Launceston 20 March, 1784 7 Brown, Thomas Exeter 24 May, 1784 7 Bradford, John Ditto 9 Jan. 1786 7 Brannegan, James Ditto 24 May, 1784 7 Bruce, Robert Ditto 24 May, 1784 7 Brown, William Ditto 24 May, 1784 7 Bryant, John Ditto 14 March, 1786 7 Brewer, William Ditto 20 March, 1786 7 Brice, William Bristol 11 Feb. 1785 7 Brand, Curtis Bryant, Michael Brand, Lucy, alias Wood London 19 July, 1786 7 Branham, Mary Ditto 23 Feb. 1785 7 Bruce, Elizabeth Ditto 10 Jan. 1787 7 Burleigh, James Ditto 7 July, 1784 7 Burn, Peter Ditto 10 Septem. 1783 7 Burne, James Ditto 21 April, 1784 7 Butler, William Ditto 7 July, 1784 7 Buckley, Joseph Dorchester 16 March, 1786 7 Burridge, Samuel Ditto 3 August, 1786 7 Burn, Patrick Burn, Simon Busley, John Bunn, Margaret London 26 April, 1786 7 Burkitt, Mary Ditto 20 August, 1786 7 Burdo, Sarah Ditto 25 Oct. 1786 7 Carver, Joseph Maidstone 13 March, 1786 7 Castle, James London 7 July, 1784 7 Campbell, James, alias George Ditto 23 Feb. 1785 7 Campbell, James Guildford 11 August, 1784 7 Carney, John Exeter 22 July, 1782 7 Carty, Francis Bodmin 14 August, 1786 7 Carey, Ann Taunton 30 March, 1786 7 Carter, Richard, alias Michael Cartwright Shrewsbury 13 March, 1784 7 Cable, Henry Carroll, Mary, wife of James Carroll London 25 Oct. 1786 7 Cesar, John Maidstone 14 March, 1785 7 Chields, William Chaddick, Thomas London 7 July, 1784 7 Church, William Dorchester 16 March, 1786 7 Chaaf, William Exeter 20 March, 1786 7 Chinery, Samuel Ditto 7 August, 1786 7 Chanin, Edward Ditto 7 August, 1786 7 Clough, Richard Durham 19 July, 1785 7 Clements, Thomas London 7 July, 1784 7 Clark, John, alias Hosier Ditto 6 April, 1785 7 Clark, William Ditto 21 April, 1784 7 Clarke, John Exeter 7 August, 1786 7 Cleaver, Mary Bristol 4 April, 1786 7 Clear, George Clark, Elizabeth Connelly, William Bristol 3 Feb. 1785 7 Cormick, Edward Hertford 2 March, 1786 7 Corden, James Warwick 21 March, 1785 7 Colling, Joseph London 7 July, 1784 7 Cole, William Ditto 7 July, 1784 7 Cox, John Matthew Ditto 23 Feb. 1785 7 Collier, Richard Kingstone 24 March, 1784 7 Connolly, William Bodmin 14 August, 1786 7 Conelly, Cornelius Exeter 7 August, 1786 7 Colman, Ishmael Dorchester 16 March, 1786 7 Coffin, John Exeter 9 Jan. 1786 7 Cole, Elizabeth Ditto 20 March, 1786 7 Cox, James Ditto 24 May, 1784 Life Copp, James Ditto 20 March, 1786 7 Coombes, Ann, wife of Samuel Coombes Taunton 30 March, 1786 7 Cole, Elizabeth London 26 April, 1786 7 Colley, Elizabeth London 23 Feb. 1785 14 Cooke, *Charlotte* Ditto 10 Jan. 1787 7 Cooper, Mary Worcester 19 July, 1785 7 Colpitts, Ann Durham 2 Oct. 1786 7 Cross, John New Sarum 25 March, 1785 7 Cropper, John London 14 Decem. 1784 7 Cross, William Coventry 21 March, 1783 7 Creamer, John Exeter 12 Jan. 1785 7 Creek, Jane London 14 Septem. 1785 7 Cunningham, Edward Ditto 7 July, 1784 7 Cullen, James Bryen Ditto 6 April, 1785 7 Cullyhorn, John Exeter 22 July, 1782 7 Cudlip, Jacob, alias Norris Bodmin 25 July, 1785 7 Cuss, John, alias Hanaboy New Sarum 11 March, 1786 7 Cuckow, William Davis, Aaron Bristol 29 March, 1785 7 Day, Richard Reading 24 July, 1786 7 Davies, Edward Stafford 27 July, 1785 7 Day, Samuel Glocester 23 March, 1785 14 Davis, Samuel Ditto 13 July, 1785 7 Davis, William Davis, James London 8 Decem. 1784 7 Daniells, Daniel Ditto 6 May, 1784 7 Daley, James Ditto 26 May, 1784 7 Davidson, John Ditto 23 Feb. 1785 7 Davis, William Brecon 15 July 1785 Life Davis Richard Daley, Ann, wife of Gore Daley, alias Ann Warburton Nether Knutsford 3 Oct1786 7 Darnell, Margaret London 18 April, 1787 7 Davis, Ann Ditto 26 April, 1786 7 Dalton, Elizabeth Ditto 14 Sept. 1785 7 Davidson, Rebecca, wife of Robert Davidson Ditto 25 Oct. 1786 7 Dawson, Margaret Ditto 10 Jan. 1787 7 Davis, Frances Chelmsford 6 March, 1786 14 Davies, Sarah Worcester 2 August, 1783 7 Davies, Mary Shrewsbury 12 March, 1785 7 Dennison, Michael Poole 15 April, 1785 7 Denison, Barnaby Bristol 30 April, 1783 7 Delany, Patrick Dickson, Thomas, alias Ralph Raw Durham 19 July, 1785 7 Discall, Timothy Bodmin 25 July, 1785 7 Dixon, Mary London 31 May, 1786 7 Dickenson, Mary Southwark 8 Jan. 1787 7 Douglas, William Lincoln 9 July, 1785 7 Dowland, Ferdinand London 23 Feb. 1785 7 Dodding, James, alias Doring Dring, William Kingston upon Hull 7 Oct. 1784 7 Dunnage, Joseph London 21 April, 1784 Life Dudgens, Elizabeth Dundass, Jane London 18 April, 1787 7 Dutton, Ann Ditto 26 April, 1786 7 Deyer, Leonard Southwark 10 Jan. 1786 7 Dykes, Mary London 26 April, 1786 7 Earle, William New Sarum 5 March, 1785 7 Eagleton, William, alias Bones Kingston 22 March,

1786 7 Eaton, Mary, alias Shephard Early, Rachel Reading 24 July, 1786 7 Eaton, Martha Eccles, Thomas Guildford 22 July, 1782 Life Edmunds, William Monmouth 21 March, 1785 7 Edwards, William Eggleston, George Maidstone 13 March, 1786 7 Ellam, Peter Ormskirk 18 July, 1785 7 Elliot, William Croydon 18 August, 1783 7 Elliot, Joseph Bristol 24 Nov. 1784 7 Ellam, Deborah Chester 30 August, 1784 7 English, Nicholas London 8 Decem. 1784 7 Everett, John Hertford 2 March, 1786 7 Everingham, Matthew London 7 July, 1784 7 Evans, Williams Shrewsbury 12 March, 1785 7 Evans, Elizabeth London 13 Decem. 1786 7 Farrell, Phillip London 15 Sep. 1784 7 Farley, William Bristol 10 Feb. 1785 7 Farmer, Ann London Fentum, Benjamin Ditto 10 Oct. 1783 7 Ferguson, John Exeter 20 March, 1786 7 Fillesey, Thomas Bristol 29 April, 1783 7 Fitzgerald, Jane, alias Phillips Ditto 4 April, 1786 7 Field, William Finlow, John, alias Hervey Field, Jane London Fitzgerald, Elizabeth Ditto 13 Decem. 1786 7 Flyn, Edward Flarty, Phebe London 21 Feb. 1787 7 Fowkes, Francis Ditto 13 Decem. 1785 7 Forrester, Robert Ditto 10 Sept. 1783 7 Foyle, William New Sarum 9 July, 1785 7 Fowles, Ann London 6 April, 1785 7 Fownes, Margaret Shrewsbury 4 August, 1784 7 Forbes, Ann Kingston 2 April, 1787 7 Freeman, James Hertford 3 March, 1784 7 Freeman, Robert London 10 Decem. 1784 7 Francis, William Ditto 14 Decem. 1784 7 Francisco, George Ditto 8 Decem. 1784 7 Fry, George Fryer, Catherine, alias Prior Fraser, William Manchester Jan. 1787 7 Fraser, Ellen Ditto Jan. 1787 7 Fuller, John Ditto 15 March, 1784 7 Gardner, Francis London 21 April, 1784 7 Garth, Edward Ditto 23 Feb. 1785 7 Garland, Francis Exeter 24 May, 1784 7 Garth, Susannah, alias Grath Gabel, Mary Southwark 13 Jan. 1784 7 Gascoygne, Olive Worcester 5 March, 1785 7 Gearing, Thomas Oxford 8 March, 1786 Life Gess, George Glocester 24 March, 1784 7 George, Anne London 11 May, 1785 7 Glenton, Thomas Northallerton 5 April, 1785 7 Gloster, William London 29 June, 1785 7 Gordon, Daniel Winchester 5 April, 1785 7 Goodwin, Edward London 21 April, 1784 7 Goodwin, Andrew Ditto 7 July, 1784 7 Gould, John Exeter 20 March, 1786 7 Gray, Charles Southwark 16 Feb. 1785 7 Griffiths, Samuel, alias Briscow, alias Butcher Gloucester 24 March, 1784 7 Greenwell, Nicholas London 10 Decem. 1784 7 Green, John Reading 11 July, 1786 7 Griffiths, Thomas London 15 Septem. 1784 7 Granger, Charles Plymouth 20 Decem. 1786 7 Grace, James Green, Hannah Groves, Mary Lincoln 9 July, 1785 7 Green, Mary London 18 August, 1787 7 Green, Ann Ditto 13 Decem. 1786 7 Greenwood, Mary Ditto 13 Decem. 1786 7 Gunter, William Bristol 4 August, 1783 7 Handford, John Winchester 1 March, 1785 7 Hatcher, John Ditto 1 March, 1785 7 Hatfield, William Maidstone 14 March, 1785 7 Hawkes, Richard Reading 28 July, 1785 7 Harris, William Maidstone 11 July, 1785 7 Hatch, John Reading 10 Jan. 1786 7 Hartley, John Oxford 2 March, 1785 7 Hart, John Stafford 27 July, 1785 7 Haines, Joseph Gloucester 13 July, 1785 7 Hathaway, Henry Ditto 24 March, 1784 7 Hayes, Dennis London 10 Decem. 1784 7 Hall, Samuel Ditto 12 March, 1785 7 Harbine, Joseph Harper, Joshua London 10 Septem. 1783 7 Hayton, George, alias Clayton Ditto 21 April, 1784 7 Harrison, Joseph Ditto 21 April, 1784 7 Hart, John Ditto 12 Jan. 1785 7 Harris, John Ditto 23 Feb. 1785 Life Hayes, John Guildford 11 August, 1784 7 Hattom, Joseph Harrison, Joseph Hamlin, William Exeter 12 Jan. 1784 7 Hall, Joseph Ditto 12 Jan. 1784 Life Hall, John Ditto 24 May, 1784 7 Hadon, John Ditto Hares, William Handy, Cooper Haynes, William Hervey, Elizabeth Hall, Margaret Hart, Frances Harrison, Mary Lincoln 6 March, 1784 7 Heading, James Chelmsford 7 March, 1785 Life Headington, Thomas Abingdon 7 July, 1785 7 Herbert, John London 21 April, 1784 7 Hart, Catherine Ditto 23 Feb. 1785 7 Herbert, John Exeter 14 March, 1786 7 Handland, Dorothy, alias Gray London 22 Feb. 1786 7 Hall, Sarah Ditto 10 Jan. 1787 7 Hamilton, Maria Ditto 19 October, 1785 7 Harrison, Mary Ditto 19 October, 1785 7 Harwood, Esther, alias Howard Ditto 20 August, 1786 7 Hayward, Elizabeth Ditto 10 Jan. 1787 7 Hall, Elizabeth Newcastle 18 Jan. 1786 7 Herbert, Jane, alias Rose, alias Jenny Russell London 30 August, 1786 7 Henry, Catherine Ditto 10 Jan. 1787 7 Hill, John Maidstone 14 March, 1785 Life Hindley, William, alias Platt Ormskirk 18 July, 1785 7 Hindle, Ottiwell Preston 6 Oct. 1785 7 Hill, John London 6 May, 1784 7 Hill, Thomas Ditto 7 July, 1784 7 Hilt, William Exeter 18 July, 1785 Life Hill, Thomas 7 Hipsley, Elizabeth London 23 Feb. 1785 7 Hill, Mary Ditto 25 Oct. 1786 7 Hollister, Job Bristol 10 Feb. 1785 7 Hawell, Thomas Stafford 5 Oct. 1785 7 Holmes, William London 7 July, 1784 7 Holloway, James Ditto 24 Aug. 1784 7 Howard, Thomas Ditto 12 Jan. 1785 7 Hogg, William Ditto 23 Feb. 1786 14 Howard, John Ditto 23 July, 1783 7 Hortop, James Exeter 20 March, 1786 7 Holland, William Ditto 7 August, 1786 7 Holmes, Susannah Hollogin, Elizabeth London 18 April, 1787 7 Hughes, Hugh Southwark 16 Feb. 1785 7 Humphrey, Edward London 8 Decem. 1784 7 Husband, William Ditto 21 April, 1784 7 Hughes, John Maidstone 15 March, 1784 7 Hurley, Jeremiah Exeter 22 July, 1782 7 Hubbard, William Humphreys, Henry Exeter 20 March, 1786 7 Hughes, Thomas Hudson, John Hussey, James Hughes, Frances Ann Lancaster 6 March, 1787 7 Hussnell, Susannah Worcester 2 Oct. 1786 7 Humphries, Mary Hylids, Thomas Guildford 1 Aug. 1784 7 Jackson, William Durham 19 July, 1785 7 Jacobs, David London 20 Oct. 1784 7 Jacobs, John Ditto 21 April, 1784 7 Jackson, Hannah Bristol 27 July, 1785 7 Jameson, James

Jackson, Jane, alias Esther Roberts London 29 June, 1785 7 Jackson, Mary Ditto 20 August, 1786 7 Jeffries, Robert Devizes 5 April, 1785 7 Jefferies, John Maidstone 11 July, 1785 7 Jenkins, Robert, alias Brown Ditto 13 March, 1786 7 Jepp, John London 10 Decem. 1784 7 Jenkins, William Exeter 20 March, 1786 7 Ingram, Benjamin London 8 Decem. 1784 7 Inett, Ann Worcester 11 March, 1786 7 Jones, Francis Winchester 12 July, 1785 7 Jones, Thomas Warwick 21 March, 1785 7 Johnson, Charles Manchester 14 April, 1785 7 Jones, Edward London 15 Septem. 1784 7 Josephs, Thomas Ditto 10 Septem. 1783 7 Johnson, William Kingston 24 March, 1784 7 Johns, Stephen Launceston 25 March, 1786 7 Jones, Margaret Ditto 8 March, 1783 14 Johnson, Edward Dorchester 16 March, 1786 7 Jones, John Exeter 24 May, 1784 14 Jones, William Shrewsbury 12 March, 1785 7 Jones, Richard Ditto 4 August, 1784 7 Jones, Thomas Bristol 30 March, 1784 14 Johnson, Catherine London 18 April, 1787 7 Johnson, Mary Ditto 26 April, 1786 7 Irvine, John, alias Aderson, alias Law Lincoln 6 March, 1784 7 Kelly, Thomas Pontefract 13 Jan. 1785 7 Kellan, John, alias Keeling London 10 Septem. 1783 Life Kennedy, Martha Kingston 2 April, 1787 7 Kidney, Thomas Bristol 20 Oct. 1783 7 Kilby, William Reading 16 Jan. 1784 7 King, John London 21 April, 1784 7 Kilpack, David Ditto 10 Septem. 1783 Life Kimberley, Edward Coventry 20 March, 1783 7 Knowler, John Maidstone 14 March, 1785 7 Knowland, Andrew Lankey, David London 26 May, 1784 7 Lane, Richard Winchester 2 March, 1784 7 Lawrell, John Bodmin 18 August, 1783 7 Lane, William Chelmsford 8 July, 1784 7 Larne, James Exeter 12 July, 1785 7 Lambeth, John Bristol 31 May, 1785 7 Lavell, Henry Lara, Flora London Laycock, Carolina Ditto Langley, Jane Ditto 14 Sept. 1785 7 Lawrence, Mary Ditto 23 Feb. 1785 7 Lemon, Isaac Chelmsford 7 March, 1785 7 Levy, Joseph London 6 May, 1784 7 Leary, John Winchester 3 March, 1783 7 Legg, George Dorchester 16 March, 1786 7 Leary, Jeremiah Bristol 30 March, 1784 14 Legrove, Stephen Lee, Elizabeth London 23 Feb. 1785 7 Lewis, Sophia Ditto 25 Oct. 1786 7 Leonard, Elizabeth Ditto 23 Feb. 1785 7 Levy, Amelia Southwark 9 Jan. 1787 7 List, George, London 10 Septem. 1783 Life Limeburner, John New Sarum 9 July, 1785 7 Limpus, Thomas Exeter 24 May, 1784 Life Lightfoot, Samuel Ditto 14 March, 1786 7 Longstreet, Joseph Marlborough 5 Oct. 1784 7 Long, Joseph Glocester 23 March, 1785 14 Lockley, John London 10 Jan. 1787 7 Long, Mary Ditto 21 Feb. 1787 Life Love, Mary Maidstone 14 March, 1785 7 Lock, Elizabeth Gloucester 26 March, 1783 7 Lucas, Nathaniel London 7 July, 1784 7 Lynch, Humphry New Sarum 25 March, 1785 7 Lynch, Ann Bristol 20 March, 1786 14 Lyde, John May, Richard New Sarum 25 March, 1785 7 Martin, Stephen Bristol 28 April, 1783 7 Mansfield, John Chelmsford 6 March, 1786 7 M'Lean, Francis Guildford 11 August, 1784 7 M'Lean, Thomas Ditto 11 August, 1784 7 Maton, Thomas Maidstone 11 July, 1785 7 M'Donnaugh, James Ditto 11 July, 1785 7 Mariner, William Oxford 8 March, 1786 7 Marrott, John Gloucester 24 March, 1784 7 M'Laughlin, Charles Durham 19 July, 1785 7 Macintire, John Ditto 19 July, 1785 7 Martin, John London 3 July, 1782 7 M'Donald, *Alexander* Ditto 10 Decem. 1784 7 Marney, William Ditto 7 July, 1784 7 Marshall, Joseph Ditto 21 April, 1784 14 M'Lean, Edward Maidstone 15 March, 1784 7 Martin, Abraham New Sarum 11 March, 1786 7 Martin, Thomas Exeter 24 May, 1784 7 Martyn, James Ditto 20 March, 1786 7 M'Cormick, Sarah Manchester 4 May, 1786 7 M'Cormack, Mary Liverpool 12 Aug. 1784 7 Mason, Betty Gloucester 23 March, 1785 14 M'Grah, Redman M'Deed, Richard M'Na Mar, William Mackrie, James Marriott, Jane London 18 April, 1787 7 Mather, Ann Ditto 18 April, 1787 7 Mather, Mather Ditto 18 April, 1787 7 Mason, Susannah, alias Gibbs Ditto M'Cabe, Eleanor Ditto 11 May, 1785 7 Marshall, Mary Ditto 23 Feb. 1785 Life Marshall, Mary Ditto 10 Jan. 1787 7 Martin, Ann Southwark 9 Jan. 1787 7 Meynell, John, alias William Radford Nottingham 10 March, 1785 7 Messiah, Jacob Meech, Jane, wife of William Meech Exeter 20 March, 1786 7 Milton, Charles Maidstone 14 March, 1785 7 Midgley, Samuel Lancaster 22 March, 1785 7 Middleton, Richard London 23 Feb. 1785 7 Mitchell Nathaniel Dorchester 3 August, 1786 7 Mills Matthew Mitchcraft, Mary Kingston 2 April, 1787 7 Mitchell, Mary Ditto 3 Oct. 1785 7 Morris, Peter Bristol 12 July, 1784 7 Mowbray, John Lincoln 5 March, 1785 7 Morgan, Richard Glocester 23 March, 1785 7 Morrisby, John London 7 July, 1784 7 Moore, William Ditto 21 Jan. 1785 7 Morley, John Ditto 21 April, 1784 7 Moorin, John Ditto 21 April, 1784 7 Morgan, Robert Ditto 6 May, 1784 7 Mobbs, Samuel Ditto 21 April, 1784 7 Morgan, William Ditto 15 Septem. 1784 7 Mould, William Guildford 11 August, 1784 7 Mollands, John Launceston 20 March, 1784 7 Moyle, Edward Ditto 19 March, 1785 7 Mood, Charles Mortimore, John Exeter 20 March, 1786 7 Morley, Joseph Morton, Mary London 23 Feb. 1785 7 Mullock, Jesse New Sarum 25 March, 1785 7 Murphy, William Liverpool 26 Jan. 1785 7 Munroe, John, alias Nurse London 21 April, 1784 7 Mullis, Stephen Exeter 12 Jan. 1785 7 Murphy, James 7 Munro, Lydia Kingston 2 April, 1787 14 Mullens, Hannah London 10 Jan. 1787 Life Nettleton, Robert Kingston upon Hull 12 October, 1784 7 Newland, John London 21 April, 1784 7 Neal, John Ditto 26 May, 1784 7 Neal, James Bristol 10 Feb. 1785 7 Needham, Elizabeth London 19 July, 1786 7 Nicholls, John Ditto 21 April, 1784 7 Norton, Phebe Ditto 25 Oct. 1786 7 Nunn, Robert

75

Ditto 7 July, 1784 7 O'Craft, John Exeter 24 May, 1784 7 Ogden, James Manchester 20 Jan. 1785 7 Okey, William Gloucester 24 March, 1784 7 Oldfield, Thomas Manchester 20 July, 1786 7 Oldfield, Isabella Ditto 20 July, 1786 7 Opley, Peter Maidstone 13 March, 1786 7 Orford, Thomas London 7 July, 1784 7 Osborne, Thomas Ditto 14 Decem. 1784 7 Osborne, Elizabeth, alias Jones Ditto 30 August, 1786 7 Owles, John Croydon 20 July, 1785 7 Owen, John London 10 Septem. 1783 7 Owen, Joseph Shrewsbury 12 March, 1785 14 Page, Paul Lincoln 11 March, 1786 7 Pane, William Nottingham 10 March, 1785 7 Parry, Edward Stafford 27 July, 1785 7 Parr, William Liverpool 17 Jan. 1785 7 Palmer, John Herry London 10 Jan. 1786 7 Parker, John Ditto 1 April, 1784 7 Parish, William Ditto 20 Oct. 1784 7 Partridge, Richard Ditto 10 Sep. 1783 Life Parris, Peter Exeter 17 March, 1783 7 Paget, Joseph Ditto 10 Jan. 1786 7 Parkinson, Jane, alias Partington, alias Ann Marsden Manchester 21 July, 1785 7 Parker, Elizabeth Gloucester 23 March, 1785 7 Parsley, Ann London 21 Feb. 1787 7 Parker, Mary Ditto 26 April, 1786 7 Partridge, Sarah, alias Roberts Ditto 23 Feb. 1785 7 Parry, Sarah Ditto 10 Jan. 1787 Life Perrot, Edward Bearcroft Bristol 3 Feb. 1785 7 Petrie, John London 14 Jan. 1784 7 Peyton, Samuel Ditto 26 May, 1785 7 Percival, Richard Ditto 7 July, 1784 7 Pettitt, John Ditto 21 April, 1784 7 Peaulet, James Ditto 7 July, 1784 7 Peet, Charles Ditto 23 Feb. 1785 Life Peck, Joshua Exeter 20 March, 1786 7 Perkins, Edward Plymouth 26 Jan. 1785 7 Petherick, John Plymouth 26 Jan. 1785 7 Penny, John 7 Phillimore, William London 10 Sept. 1783 7 Phillips, Richard Ditto 10 Decem. 1783 7 Phillips, Mary Taunton 30 March, 1786 7 Phyfield, Roger, alias Twyfield Shrewsbury 12 March, 1785 7 Phyn, Mary London 14 Septem. 1785 7 Pigott, Samuel Exeter 20 March, 1786 7 Pinder, Mary Lincoln 13 Jan. 1787 7 Pipkin, Elizabeth London 7 Piles, Mary Ditto 6 April, 1785 7 Pope, David Southwark 16 Feb. 1785 7 Power, John London 14 Decem. 1786 7 Pontie, John Ditto 23 Feb. 1785 Life Poole, Jane Wells 19 August, 1786 7 Power, William Powley, Elizabeth Powell, Ann London 13 Decem. 1786 7 Price, John Southwark 16 Feb. 1785 7 Prior, Thomas Reading 16 Jan. 1784 7 Price, James Gloucester 13 July, 1785 7 Pritchard, Thomas Pugh, Edward Gloucester 5 Oct. 1784 7 Randall, John Manchester 14 April, 1785 7 Reymond, George London 12 Jan. 1785 7 Ramsey, John Kingston 24 March, 1784 7 Repeat, Charles Warwick 21 March, 1785 7 Read, William Croydon 18 August, 1783 7 Reardon, Bartholemew Winchester 15 July, 1783 7 Read, Ann London 23 Feb. 1785 Life Risdale, Thomas, alias Crowder Bristol 29 March, 1785 Life Richard, James East Grinstead 20 March, 1786 7 Richardson, James Maidstone 14 March, 1785 7 Risby, Edward Gloucester 24 March, 1784 7 Richardson, William London 10 Decem. 1784 7 Richardson, Hardwicke Ditto 25 Oct. 1785 7 Richardson, John Ditto 7 July, 1784 7 Richard, David Ditto 26 May, 1784 7 Richardson, Samuel Ditto 15 Septem. 1784 7 Rickson, William Chelmsford 8 July, 1784 7 Richards, John, alias Williams Winchester 2 March, 1784 7 Richard, James Launceston 25 March, 1786 7 Rice, John Exeter 18 July, 1785 7 Rope, Anthony Chelmsford 7 March, 1785 7 Rogers, Daniel Croydon 20 July, 1785 7 Robinson, George Lincoln 9 July, 1785 7 Rogers, Isaac Gloucester 23 March, 1785 14 Robinson, Thomas Kingston upon Hull 7 Oct. 1784 7 Robert, John Liverpool 26 Jan. 1785 7 Robinson, George London 21 April, 1784 7 Romain, John, Ditto 15 Septem. 1784 7 Rowe, John Launceston 19 March, 1785 7 Rowe, William Ditto 19 March, 1785 7 Roberts, William Bodmin 14 August, 1786 7 Robinson, William Exeter 24 May, 1784 7 Roach, Henry Ditto 24 May, 1784 7 Robins, John, alias Major Ditto 18 July, 1785 7 Rous, Walton, alias Batley Rolt, Mary London Rosson, Isabella Ditto 10 Jan. 1787 7 Russel, John Ditto 21 April, 1784 7 Ruglass, John Ditto 23 Feb. 1785 Life Russler, John Ditto 23 Feb. 1785 Life Ruce, James Bodmin 29 July, 1782 7 Ruth, Robert Exeter 14 March, 1786 7 Ryan, John Saltmarsh, William Kingston 28 March, 1785 7 Sanderson, Thomas Lincoln 9 July, 1785 7 Sands, William Ditto 9 July, 1785 7 Sampson, Peter London 7 July, 1784 7 Sandlin, Ann, alias Lynes, alias Pattens Ditto 13 Decem. 1786 7 Scattergood, Robert Stafford 6 Oct. 1785 7 Scott, Elizabeth London 21 Feb. 1787 7 Selshire, Samuel Ditto 21 April, 1784 7 Seymour, John Sherborne 25 April, 1786 7 Shearman, William Reading 7 Oct. 1785 7 Shaw, Joseph Stafford 27 July, 1785 7 Shepherd, Robert Durham 19 July, 1785 7 Sharpe, George Ditto 19 July, 1785 7 Shore, William Lancaster 22 March, 1785 7 Shore, John Shiers, James London 23 Feb. 1785 Life Silverthorn, John New Sarum 6 March, 1784 7 Sideway, Robert Slater, Sarah London 23 Feb. 1785 7 Smart, Richard Gloucester 10 Jan. 1786 7 Smart, Daniel Ditto 10 Jan. 1786 7 Smith, Thomas Lancaster 22 March, 1785 7 Smith, William Liverpool 26 Jan. 1785 7 Smith, Edward London 15 Oct. 1784 7 Smith, William Ditto 10 April, 1783 7 Smith, Thomas, alias Haynes Ditto 21 April, 1784 7 Smith, James Ditto 23 Feb. 1785 7 Smith, John Guildford 11 August, 1784 7 Smith, William Bodmin 25 July, 1785 7 Smith, Ann, wife of John Smith Winchester 1 March, 1785 7 Smith, Hannah Ditto 5 April, 1785 7 Smith, William Dorchester 16 March, 1786 7 Smith, Edward Exeter 14 March, 1786 7 Smith, John Ditto 14 March, 1786 7 Small, John Ditto 14 March, 1786 7 Smith, Ann London 18 April, 1787 7 Smith, Catherine Ditto 18 April, 1787 7 Smith, Ann Ditto 30 August, 1786 7 Smith, Catherine Ditto 10 Jan. 1787 7 Smith, Mary Ditto 10 Jan. 1787 7 Snaleham, William Ditto 21 April, 1784 7 Sparks, Henry Spencer, Daniel Dorchester

76

3 August, 1786 14 Spencer, John, alias Pearce Spence, Mary Wigan Jan. 1786 5 Sprigmore, *Charlotte* London 19 August, 1785 7 Springham, Mary Ditto 25 October, 1786 7 Squires, James Kingston 11 April, 1785 7 Stanley, William New Sarum 25 March, 1785 7 Strong, James Dorchester 10 March, 1784 7 Stow, James Lincoln 9 July, 1785 7 Stone, Martin Warwick 21 March, 1785 7 Stokee, John Durham 19 July, 1785 7 Stone, Charles London 10 Decem. 1784 7 Stone, Henry Ditto 10 Decem. 1784 7 Stogdell, John Ditto 20 Decem. 1784 14 Stuart, James Ditto 21 April, 1784 7 Stanton, Thomas, alias Ebden Launceston 20 March, 1784 7 Stephens, John Morris Dorchester 16 March, 1786 7 Stewart, Margaret Exeter 28 August, 1786 7 Strech, Thomas Shrewsbury 16 August, 1783 7 Summers, John Gloucester 13 July, 1784 7 Taylor, Joshua Manchester 14 Oct. 1784 7 Taylor, Henry Taylor, Sarah Kingston 2 April, 1787 7 Tenant, Thomas Hilton, alias Phillip Divine Chelmsford 6 March, 1786 7 Teague, Cornelius Bodmin 25 July, 1785 7 Tenchall, James, alias Tenninghill Thompson, William Durham 19 July, 1785 7 Thomas, James London 10 Decem. 1784 7 Thompson, James Ditto 7 July, 1784 7 Thomas, James Ditto 10 Septem. 1783 7 Thomas, John Ditto 21 April, 1784 7 Thompson, William Ditto 26 May, 1784 7 Thackery, Elizabeth Manchester 4 May, 1786 7 Thoudy, James Thomas, Elizabeth Wigan Jan. 1787 7 Thornton, Ann London 13 Decem. 1786 7 Tunmins, Thomas Warwick 21 March, 1785 7 Tilley, Thomas Stafford 27 July, 1785 7 Till, Thomas London 23 Feb. 1785 7 Todd, Nicholas Ditto 21 April, 1784 7 Trotter, Joseph Maidstone 13 March, 1786 7 Trace, John Exeter 20 March, 1786 7 Trippett, Susannah London 20 August, 1786 7 Turner, Ralph Manchester 14 April, 1785 7 Tuso, Joseph London 23 Feb. 1785 Life Turner, John Tucker, Moses Plymouth 7 June, 1786 7 Turner, Thomas Turner, John Turner, Mary Worcester 5 March, 1785 7 Twyneham, William Reading 10 Jan. 1786 7 Twyfield, Ann, since said to be married to William Dawley,   a convict Shrewsbury 4 August, 1784 7 Tyrrell, William Winchester 1 March, 1785 7 Vandell, Edward East Grinstead 22 March, 1784 7 Vincent, Henry London 21 April, 1784 7 Vickery, William Exeter 20 March, 1786 7 Underwood, James New Sarum 11 March, 1786 14 Usher, John Maidstone 14 March, 1785 7 Waterhouse, William Kingston 28 March, 1785 7 Watsan, John Maidstone 13 March, 1786 7 Ward, John Lowth 11 July, 1786 7 Wall, William Oxford 8 March, 1786 7 Wager, Benjamin London 20 Oct. 1784 7 Walsh, William Ditto 15 Septem. 1784 7 Walker, John Ditto 20 Oct. 1784 7 Walbourne, James Ditto 10 Septem. 1783 7 Watson, Thomas Exeter 20 March, 1786 7 Ware, *Charlotte* Watkins, Mary Wainwright, Ellen, alias Estther Eccles Preston Jan. 1787 7 Ward, Ann London 19 Decem. 1786 7 Wade, Mary, alias Cacklane Ditto 19 July, 1786 14 Welch, James Maidstone 14 March, 1785 7 Welch, John Durham 19 July, 1785 7 West, Benjamin London 10 Decem. 1784 7 Westwood, John Ditto 20 October, 1784 7 Welch, John Ditto 26 May, 1784 7 Welch, John Ditto 10 Septem. 1783 Life Westlale, Edward Exeter 20 March, 1786 7 Waddicomb, Richard Ditto 20 March, 1786 7 Wheeler, Samuel Croydon 20 July, 1785 7 Whitaker, George Maidstone 14 March, 1785 7 Whiting, William Gloucester 23 March, 1785 7 Whitton, Edward Maidstone 10 March, 1783 Life White, James Ditto 11 August, 1783 7 Wilcocks, Samuel Dorcester 10 March, 1784 7 Wilton, William Bristol 12 Jan. 1784 7 Wilson, Peter Manchester 20 Jan. 1785 7 Wilson, John Wigan 10 Oct. 1785 7 Williams, Charles London 7 July, 1784 7 Williams, James Ditto 11 May, 1785 7 Wilson, Charles Ditto 10 Septem. 1783 Life Williams, John, alias Black Jack Maidstone 2 August, 1784 7 Williams, Robert Launceston 25 March, 1786 7 Williams, John, alias Floyd Bodmin 18 August, 1783 7 Wilding, John, alias Warren Bury 23 March, 1784 7 Wickham, Mary New Sarum 2 August, 1788 14 Williams, Peter, alias Flaggett, alias Creamer Exeter 24 May, 1784 7 Wilcocks, Richard Ditto 20 March, 1786 7 Williams, John Ditto 7 August, 1786 7 Wisehammer, John Bristol 10 Feb. 1785 7 Williams, Daniel Preston 23 March, 1785 7 Williams, Frances Mold 2 Septem. 1783 7 Williams, Mary London 22 Feb. 1786 7 Wood, George Ditto 20 Oct. 1784 7 Woodcock, Peter Ditto 7 July, 1784 7 Woodham, Samuel Ditto 23 Feb. 1785 Life Worsdell, William Launceston 22 March, 1783 7 Woolcot, John Exeter 18 July, 1785 Life Woodcock, Francis Shrewsbury 13 March, 1784 7 Wood, Mark Wright, Thomas Reading 28 Feb. 1785 7 Wright, Benjamin London 6 May, 1784 7 Wright, Joseph Ditto 26 May, 1784 7 Wright, William Ditto 15 Sept. 1783 7 Wright, James Maidstone 11 August, 1783 7 Wright, Ann London 23 Feb. 1785 7 Yardsley, Thomas, Shrewsbury 4 August, 1784 7 Yates, Nancy York 9 July, 1785 7 Young, John London 20 Oct. 1784 7 Young, Simon Ditto 23 Feb. 1785 7 Youngson, Elizabeth Lancaster 6 March, 1787 7 Youngson, George Ditto 6 March, 1787 7

The End

Made in the USA
Las Vegas, NV
06 April 2022

46980893R00046